THE
PERSIAN
GULF
CRISIS
AND THE FINAL FALL OF BABYLON

D1466720

THE
PERSIAN GULF
CRISIS
AND THE FINAL FALL OF BABYLON

N.W. HUTCHINGS

Hearthstone Publishing Ltd.

P.O. Box 815 · Oklahoma City, Ok 73101

A Division Of
Southwest Radio Church Of The Air

All scripture references are from the King James Version unless otherwise stated.

Printed in the United States of America

Published by:
Hearthstone Publishing
P.O. Box 815
Oklahoma City, OK 73101

Library of Congress Catalog Card Number 90-84546
ISBN 0-9624517-6-2

Contents

The City 10

Babylon B.C. 20

Babylon's Fall and Decline 30

Babylon the Harlot 41

Babylon In the Church 52

The Babylonian Priesthood 62

U.S.A. and Babylon 72

Iraq — Prelude To Armageddon 83

Isaiah Against Babylon 102

Jeremiah Against Babylon 110

John Against Babylon 121

The World Beyond Babylon 128

Introduction

It is claimed by educators that man's knowledge is doubling every two and a half years.

It is claimed by science that ninety percent of all scientists who ever lived are alive today.

Man's speed of travel for thousands of years remained constant, about thirty miles per hour. In just ninety years, travel speed has increased to one hundred miles per hour on the ground, one thousand miles per hour in the air, and twenty thousand miles per hour in outer space.

In the last ninety years radio, television, laser, and satellite communications have been developed.

In the past fifty years nuclear weapons capable of destroying the world many times over have been developed.

In the twentieth century earthquakes and famines have greatly accelerated in frequency and victims.

Computers have been so developed and implemented that practically the entire world is identified by numbers, and labor, buying, and selling use code marks and numbers.

Theft, robbery, rape, and murder are increasing to the point that the whole world is filled with violence, as in the days of Noah. Immorality abounds and crime is out of control. An increasing percentage of the population live together without civil or church authority, and of those who do marry, over fifty percent get a divorce.

In spite of the great advance in medical science (organ transplants, health programs, miracle germ-fighting drugs, vaccinations against disease), pestilences like heart disease, cancer, herpes, and AIDS infect increasing millions.

After almost two thousand years, Israel became a sovereign nation again in 1948. Jews in Israel today pray for the coming of Messiah and the rebuilding of the Temple.

Europe is scheduled to become a federated nation again in 1992.

President George Bush and others now hail the United Nations as holding the promise of a New World Order in the near future.

The ancient city of Babylon is being restored. Babylon (modern Iraq) is led by a dictator who claims to be a reincarnation of Nebuchadnezzar. Iraq, a relatively small and insignificant nation, now threatens one-half of the world's oil supply and attained such power that it challenges the entire world.

Armies from all over the world gather in the Middle East where the Association for Atomic Scientists predicted in 1984 the exact scenario for Armageddon.

Are all of the above the fulfilling of prophecy related to the second coming of Jesus Christ? Or, are they all simply a maze of unexplained coincidence?

I believe the former, and in this book, I go back into

the history of Babylon, both biblical and historical, to present our conviction that everything that is occurring in the Persian Gulf and the Middle East today was foretold by the prophets of the only true God thousands of years ago. If the reader believes we have presented sufficient evidence to support our conclusion, then he or she should take account of their readiness to meet the Lord at His coming and escape the great and terrible day of God Almighty.

Preface

The first edition of this book was written and published soon after the invasion of Kuwait by the armed forces of Iraq in August 1990. At the writing of this preface, airplanes of the U.N. forces in Saudi Arabia and the Persian Gulf area are attacking military targets in Iraq and Scud missiles from Iraq have exploded in the Tel Aviv area.

In reviewing the developments of the Persian Gulf crisis looking forward to the "final fall of Babylon," we refer to Isaiah 13:1-7: *"The burden of Babylon, which Isaiah the son of Amoz did see. Lift ye up a banner upon the high mountain, exalt the voice unto them, shake the hand, that they may go into the gates of the nobles. I have commanded my sanctified ones, I have also called my mighty ones for mine anger, even them that rejoice in my highness. The noise of a multitude in the mountains, like as of a great people; a tumultuous noise of the kingdoms of nations gathered together: the Lord of hosts mustereth the host of the battle. They come from a far country, from the end of heaven, even the Lord, and the weapons of his indignation, to destroy the whole land. Howl ye; for the day of the Lord is at hand; it shall come as a destruction from the Almighty. Therefore shall all hands be faint, and every man's heart shall melt."*

This prophecy could not refer to the first fall of Babylon in 545 B.C. because only two nearby nations, Media and Persia, were involved in the capture of Babylon, almost without a fight. What we see today is a coalition of eighteen nations, some thousands of miles away on the other side of the earth. They have gathered with sufficient weapons to destroy Babylon as the prophecy indicates.

Even while diplomatic efforts by the Arab league, the United Nations, nations of the European Common Market, and other independent peace moves were launched to reduce the developing crisis, millions of foreigners in Kuwait and Iraq frantically were fleeing the country. There seemed to be a sixth sense, so to speak, that there was impending disaster:

"The voice of them that flee and escape out of the land of Babylon, to declare in Zion the vengeance of the Lord our God, the vengeance of his temple . . . Flee out of the midst of Babylon, and deliver every man his soul: be not cut off in her iniquity; for this is the time of the Lord's vengeance; he will render unto her a recompence" (Jer. 50:28; 51:6).

God has never forgiven Babylon for the destruction of the temple of the Lord in Jerusalem, and what is happening in Iraq at the writing of this preface is, as we believe, the carrying out of His vengeance for something that Babylon did over twenty-five hundred years ago.

It has been the consensus of pre-millennial, pre-tribulation prophetic scholars that the final destruction of Babylon will occur during the tribulation period. But let us notice again the exact wording of Isaiah 13:6: *"Howl ye; for the day of the Lord is at hand. . . ."* In other words, when the armies of many nations begin the war with Babylon, the world is to know that the "day of the Lord," the tribulation period of seven years is at hand, meaning very near. The verses in Isaiah 13 after the seventh verse, do relate to the tribulation.

It would then seem, that if what we observe in the Persian Gulf today is the beginning of the fulfillment of the prophecies of Isaiah 13; Jeremiah 50,51; Revelation 17,18; then we are indeed living in the extremity of the age, and the coming of the Lord is very near, even at the door.

Chapter One

The City

The unfolding of the chronological course of prophecy to its ultimate conclusion can be compared to a Shakespearean drama where all the main actors in the play emerge once more at the final scene to make a last curtain call. As we look to Europe and the Middle East, we see the Common Market as evidence of the revived Roman Empire; the biblical nations of Syria, Egypt, Ethiopia, Greece, Iran (or Persia), Arabia, and Gog (or Russia), are in their proper prophetic places. Israel is back in the Land of Promise. We also see Jordan, comprising the ancient nations of Ammon, Moab, and Edom, ready to fulfill its destiny during the Great Tribulation as prophesied by Daniel. But what about one of the most powerful empires that was prominent in biblical times, the nation that was the very genesis of the "times of the Gentiles," Babylon?

It is certain that Babylon is to play a major role in world events during the last days. From chapters fifty through fifty-two of Jeremiah, and chapters seventeen through nineteen in the Book of Revelation, Babylon is mentioned during the Great Tribulation as being a city, a nation, a commercial power, and a religious system.

There is no mystery about Israel being established again as a nation in 1948; there is no mystery about Syria, Egypt, or the other nations in their end-time setting. So why is the identity of Babylon in the last days called a mystery? It would seem that it is called a mystery because its various identities are hidden from the general understanding of the world.

Perhaps the least mysterious aspect of the multi-faceted Babylon of the last days is the city itself. But even so, as we see the attempt being made to restore this ancient metropolis to its former glory, most biblical and historical scholars doubt and wonder that this can ever be accomplished. In 1971 plans were announced by Iraq to rebuild Babylon according to its ancient architectural designs. Funds for the project were to be provided by Iraq, UNESCO, and the Arab oil barons of the Middle East. When we were in Babylon in 1978, the ruins were being excavated, and the theatre of Nebuchadnezzar had been restored, as well as several of the temples and other buildings.

Two years after we were in Babylon, the war between Iraq and Iran erupted, and continued for eight years. Although the war slowed the rebuilding of Babylon, it was not entirely stopped. The January 16, 1987 edition of *The Los Angeles Times* included an article entitled, "New Writing On Wall — CAN BABYLON RELIVE ITS GLORY DAYS?" I quote:

> " '*In the same hour came forth fingers of a man's hand, and wrote . . . upon the plaster of*

the wall of the king's palace . . . And this is the writing that was written . . . God hath numbered thy kingdom, and finished it . . . Thou art weighed in the balances, and art found wanting' (Dan. 5).

"There is still handwriting on the wall of Nebuchadnezzar's palace. Not as apocalyptic as the message that the Bible says Daniel translated for King Belshazzar, it simply proclaims to all who pass through the portals of these time-worn ruins that 'Pete was here.' Today, little remains of the grandeur that was ancient Babylon, the city of Hammurabi and Nebuchadnezzar, the site of the Hanging Gardens and the Tower of Babel, and, of course, the place where the famous handwriting on the wall spoiled Belshazzar's dinner party. Nowadays graffiti deface what is left of the walls. . . . In a way, it is perversely fitting. In the reconstructed Temple of Emach, graffiti in a veritable Babel of languages clutter the restored white-washed walls. . . .

"The present intrudes upon Babylon in others ways too. At the entrance to the ruins, next to a half-size model of the great Ishtar Gate, stands a thirty-foot-high portrait of Iraqi President Saddam Hussein, shown there as a modern-day Nebuchadnezzar protecting Babylon from its past and present enemies, the Persians of neighboring Iran. At a time when

Iraq is hard-pressed to continue paying for the cost of its six-year-old war with Iran, Hussein has ordered that no expense be spared to restore ancient Babylon to its former glory in time for an international music festival that is scheduled to be held here in September. The restoration project, begun in 1978 before the start of the Iran-Iraq War, was undertaken to save the remnants of the city. . . .

"However, Babylon has assumed additional importance for the government since the war broke out in September 1980. Keen on establishing a link between its current conflict with the Persians and the legendary battles of the past, the Iraqi government has speeded up the reconstruction in order to make Babylon a symbol of national pride. In the haste, however, some Western critics suggest that Babylon is not so much being restored to its former glory as it is being turned into a three-dimensional propaganda statement. . . .

"Iraqi officials bridle at criticism like this and say when the reconstruction is finished, the new Babylon will look just like the old one. . . .

" 'Many, many things have been stolen from Babylon,' said Munir Bashir, an internationally known musician who is supervising the organization of the Babylon Music Festival. 'We have asked for these things back, but it is

impossible,' he added regretfully. Bashir, who plays the lute and the ud, has ambitious plans for the music festival to be held in the restored amphitheater and other made-over parts of the two thousand-year-old ruins from September 22 to October 22. 'We will have musicians from all over the world, from Europe, Asia, Africa, and Arabia. From America we will have a famous movie star — I cannot say which one yet — and we have asked for Madonna,' he said.

"Why Madonna? 'Because the Iraqi young people love Madonna. Madonna lives here with the Iraqi people,' he added, pointing to his heart. 'I hope Madonna will know this fact and will come.'

"U.S. officials, hoping that a still-active cultural exchange program with Iraq can keep alive relations that fell into something of a political coma after the disclosures of U.S. arms sales to Iran, are trying to recruit American talent for the festival. However, Western diplomats express concern that the Iraqis may be in for a disappointment when it comes to getting big-name U.S. talent. 'The Iraqis want this to be a great festival, like Baalbek in the old days,' one diplomat said. 'But with the war on, a lot of people are going to be afraid to come.'

"Bashir dismisses these fears as unfounded,

noting that Babylon, fifty-five miles south of Baghdad on the Euphrates River, is well away from any fighting and has never been bombed. 'Babylon is completely safe,' he said. Also, 'this is not just an Iraqi festival,' he added, warming to his favorite subject. 'It is a festival for the whole world, because Babylon was the capital of civilization once and has given the world so much. People from all over want to come to Babylon.'

"Talent already signed up for the festival includes ballet troupes from the Soviet Union and France, opera from Italy, folk dancers from Greece, Turkey, Poland, and Yugoslavia, flamenco artists from Spain and Bedouin dancers from Saudi Arabia.

" 'The movie stars who are our guests will each recite the laws of Hammurabi in their own languages,' Bashir said. 'Everything will be like it was in ancient Babylon,' he added. 'People will be given Babylonian costumes to wear and newly minted Babylonian money to spend.' Even the food to be served will be based on two thousand-year-old recipes, he said.

"The Babylon . . . construction workers are rebuilding . . . the Babylon of Nebuchadnezzar, who reigned from 605 to 562 B.C. . . .

"The city rising somewhat hurriedly from the ruins in time for the festival is also the one that got such bad reviews in the Bible as the

'mother of harlots and of earth's abominations,'
a reputation that Bashir says is unfair. . . . And
although he does not think of it in quite these
terms, what Bashir really wants to do is to
prove that the Bible was wrong. For in bringing
together musicians from around the world to
perform here, Bashir is attempting to grant
Babylon a pardon from the biblical sentence
imposed upon it in the Book of Revelation,
when a 'mighty angel cast a stone into the sea
and said: So shall Babylon the great city be
thrown down with violence, and shall be found
no more: and the sound of harpers and
minstrels, of flute players and trumpeters, shall
be heard in thee no more.' "

Why would Saddam Hussein designate millions of
dollars to the rebuilding of an old city that has apparently
no commercial or social value, especially in the midst of
a war? The possible answer to this question may be in a
resurgence of Chaldean pride, as Saddam Hussein
insisted. But the most definitive reason has to be so that
Babylon will be destroyed like Sodom and Gomorrah
just before Jesus Christ returns.

The items of importance contained in *The Los
Angeles Times* story about the 1987 music festival in
Babylon are:

1. A huge portrait of Saddam Hussein stands beside the
   Ishtar Gate.

2. A command world music festival was chosen to announce the rebirth of Babylon.
3. No expense was to be spared in restoring Babylon to its former glory.
4. The American rock star, Madonna, was specifically requested to be the queen of the festival.
5. They are seeking proof that God is a liar for saying that Babylon would be destroyed in a fiery holocaust.

Babylon was built on the ancient site of Babel, and it was at Babel that the people decided that God was wrong when He commanded them to spread over the face of the earth. They said, "Let us build a tower to heaven and defy God." Nebuchadnezzar defied God, and he was made to eat grass in the fields for seven years until he acknowledged that God was the Most High of both Heaven and earth. Belshazzar defied God and defiled the holy vessels taken from the Temple in Jerusalem. Babylon is a historical symbol of man's defiance of the Lord of Heaven; therefore, it is no surprise that one reason for this modern Belshazzar-type festival was to defy God's judgment already determined in His Word.

From the Scriptures we know there is music that praises and pleases God. We read in Psalm 150: *"Praise ye the Lord, Praise God in his sanctuary: praise him in the firmament of his power. Praise him for his mighty acts: praise him according to his excellent greatness. Praise him with the sound of the trumpet: praise him with the psaltery and harp. Praise him with the timbrel and dance: praise him with stringed instruments and organs. Praise him upon the loud cymbals: praise him upon the high sounding cymbals. Let every thing that hath breath praise the Lord. Praise ye the Lord."*

There is also music that is an abomination to God. When Moses came down from Mt. Sinai with the law of God graven on tablets of stone, he heard the sound of such music in the camp of Israel and knew before he arrived at the camp that the people were defying God and worshipping an idol.

The same kind of satanic music was heard in ancient Babylon when Nebuchadnezzar commanded the people who came from all over the empire to fall down and worship his golden image. We read in Daniel 3:14-15, *"Nebuchadnezzar spake and said unto them, Is it true, O Shadrach, Meshach, and Abednego, do not ye serve my gods, nor worship the golden image which I have set up? Now if ye be ready that at what time ye hear the sound of the cornet, flute, harp, sackbut, psaltery, and dulcimer, and all kinds of musick, ye fall down and worship the image which I have made; well: but if ye worship not, ye shall be cast the same hour into the midst of a burning fiery furnace; and who is that God that shall deliver you out of my hands?"*

It is thought that this idol was erected just to the south of Babylon on a foundational pedestal which is still there. The theatre of Nebuchadnezzar was also on the south side of Babylon outside the walls of the city. So it was probably in the king's theatre where the musicians played when everyone fell down and worshipped the idol. It seems more than just coincidental that it was in the same theatre that the Babylonian music festival was convened on September 22, 1987. With interest we note that Nebuchadnezzar stated that at his music festival there was "all kinds of musick." At the Babylonian music festival in 1987 there was all kinds of music from all over the world, everything from opera to rock music.

In the eighteenth chapter of Revelation, the ultimate and final destruction of the city of Babylon is prophesied — it will be destroyed in one hour with a mighty fiery judgment. We read of the fate of the musicians of Babylon in Revelation 18:20-22, *"Rejoice over her, thou heaven, and ye holy apostles and prophets; for God hath avenged you on her. And a mighty angel took up a stone like a great millstone, and cast it into the sea, saying, Thus with violence shall that great city Babylon be thrown down, and shall be found no more at all. And the voice of harpers, and musicians, and of pipers, and trumpeters, shall be heard no more at all in thee. . . ."*

The question of contemporary consideration is whether the Babylon on the Euphrates that has been in a process of restoration for the past twenty years is the Babylon mentioned in Isaiah 13; Jeremiah 50 and 51; and in Revelation 18 and 19 that will be destroyed as were Sodom and Gomorrah in one hour. We will approach this question in more detail, from both the perspective of the 1990 Middle East crisis, and the prophetic Word, in later chapters.

Chapter Two

Babylon B.C.

As we have noted in the previous chapter, the 1987 celebration in Babylon was for the purpose of letting all the world know that Babylon lives again and that God is wrong in His pronouncement of judgment against the city in the last days.

The beginning of the biblical history of Babylon is recorded in Genesis 11:1-9: *"And the whole earth was of one language, and of one speech. And it came to pass, as they journeyed from the east, that they found a plain in the land of Shinar; and they dwelt there. And they said one to another, Go to, let us make brick, and burn them throughly. And they had brick for stone, and slime had they for morter. And they said, Go to, let us build us a city and a tower, whose top may reach unto heaven; and let us make us a name, lest we be scattered abroad upon the face of the whole earth. And the Lord came down to see the city and the tower, which the children of men builded. And the Lord said, Behold, the people is one, and they have all one language; and this they begin to do: and now nothing will be restrained from them, which they have imagined to do. Go to, let us go down, and there confound their language, that they may not under-*

stand one another's speech. So the Lord scattered them abroad from thence upon the face of all the earth: and they left off to build the city. Therefore is the name of it called Babel; because the Lord did there confound the language of all the earth: and from thence did the Lord scatter them abroad upon the face of all the earth."

The setting for the building of the Tower of Babel was between the time of the flood and the birth of Abraham, about 2200 B.C. As the descendants of Noah multiplied, as described in Genesis 10, they began to migrate outward to other lands as God had commanded. But then the people came to the land of Shinar, later called Mesopotamia or Chaldea. This flat plain lies between the Tigris and Euphrates rivers, between Babylon and Baghdad, and extends southward about three hundred miles to the Persian Gulf. Many think of this area as a semi-desert region, but it is actually one of the most fertile lands in the world. The soil is deep and rich, and a network of canals from the Tigris and Euphrates provide water for irrigation. In the spring season, abundant crops of fruits and vegetables stretch as far as the eye can see. This rich land became the economic foundation for Sumer, Chaldea, Assyria, and Babylon.

When the people after the flood came to this fertile land, they decided to settle there, because it would provide everything they would need. But we read in Genesis 10:25 that it was also during this time, the days of Peleg, that the land mass of the earth was broken up and divided. Scientists contend that the separation of the islands and continents occurred millions of years ago, but according to the Bible, it was only about four thousand years ago. The fear of being scattered over the face of the earth as a result of the dividing of the earth could have motivated the building of the Tower of Babel. The objective was to keep the people in one place by building a tower whose top would reach into the heavens. Some Bible scholars believe the interpretation should be that a tower was to be constructed with Heaven at the top. The people of the Chaldean civilization were worshippers of the moon god, Nannar. Altars and sacrificial places of worship were located on top of the ziggurats and temples at Ur, Nineveh, and Babylon.

It is interesting to notice that the Tower of Babel was made of brick with slime for mortar. The slime pits are still prevalent today in Babylon. The slime is a thick oil, or semi-asphalt, the residue of oil seepage that rises to the surface from oil deposits deep in the ground. There are numerous oil fields today in Iraq between Babylon and the Persian Gulf.

The walls of the buildings of Nineveh were made of stone because that great city is in the mountains about two hundred miles north of Baghdad. But on the lower plains of Mesopotamia, there are no stones. The cities of Babylon and Ur were made of brick, which we are told in the Bible were baked thoroughly. Even after four thousand years, these bricks are still solid, much better than bricks made today. Between Baghdad and Babylon there are many brick furnaces today, where bricks are being made for the rebuilding of Babylon. Ancient Babylon was constructed from hundreds of millions of bricks made in the furnaces of Nebuchadnezzar. These furnaces were also used to cremate many of the Jews taken into captivity. While Meshach, Abednego, and Shadrach escaped the furnace, others did not. We read in Jeremiah 29:22, *"And of them shall be taken up a curse by all the captivity of Judah which are in Babylon, saying, The Lord make thee like Zedekiah and like Ahab, whom the king of Babylon roasted in the fire."* So Hitler was not the first Jew-hater who burned them in furnaces.

In settling this region after the flood, the people saw the land was not only fertile and abundant in vegetation, but biblical historians have noted that large herds of deer, elk, and antelope found a natural habitat in the area. This food source for predatory beasts resulted in the land between the Tigris and Euphrates rivers being overrun by lions, tigers, and leopards, which were a constant danger. Therefore we read in Genesis 10:8-10, *"And Cush begat Nimrod: he began to be a mighty one in the earth. He was a mighty hunter before the Lord: wherefore it is said, Even as Nimrod the mighty hunter before the Lord. And the beginning of his kingdom was Babel, and Erech, and Accad, and Calneh, in the land of Shinar."*

A conclusion from this Scripture is that Nimrod launched hunting expeditions to rid the land of these fierce beasts. Inscriptions and pictorial accounts in brick and stone in the ruins of Nineveh and Babylon reveal that Assyria and Babylonian kings hunted and killed these wild animals. From Nimrod doubtless came the tradition that kings should also be great hunters. It has been noted by some authorities of the Hebrew text that Genesis 10:9 could also be interpreted, *"He was a mighty hunter who stood against the Lord: wherefore it is said, Even as Nimrod the mighty hunter against the Lord."* Nimrod used his reputation, as the mighty hunter who saved the people, to lead them to defy God.

The *Jewish Encyclopedia* says of Nimrod:

> *"He who made all the people rebellious against God."*

Josephus wrote:

> *"Now it was Nimrod who excited them to such an affront and contempt of God. . . . He also gradually changed the government into tyranny, seeing no other way of turning men from the fear of God . . . the multitudes were very ready to follow the determination of Nimrod . . . and they built a tower, neither sparing any pain, nor being in any degree negligent about the work: and, by reason of the multitude of hands employed in it, it grew very high. . . . The place wherein they built the tower is now called Babylon."*

After the confusion of the language spoken at Babel, and the death of Nimrod, the Middle East became ruled by city-states. Hammurabi, called

Amraphel in Genesis 14, was king over Shinar and Babylon. Hammurabi is given a notable place in history for a code of laws, but a note in the Pilgrim Bible on Genesis 14:1 states of this early Babylonian king:

> *"Amraphel . . . is another name for the Hammurabi of ancient history who drew up the first code of laws. His laws were very often unjust, deliberately favoring rich men and oppressing the poor. Though there are many parallels between this code and the law which God gave later to Israel through Moses, there are also many contrasts, and the latter law is far superior."*

Hammurabi made an alliance with four other northern city-states and invaded the cities to the south which included Petra, Sodom, and Gomorrah. Lot and his household living at Sodom were taken captive. When Abraham, who at the time had pitched his tents on the plains of Mamre, received the news, he immediately armed his servants, a force of three hundred eighteen men, and gave chase. He caught up with Hammurabi near Damascus and defeated him and his allies. Abraham rescued Lot and his household and recaptured all the spoils of war that had been taken.

The strongest nation to rise up out of the territories ruled by Nimrod to seriously threaten Israel was Assyria. The capital of Assyria was Nineveh on the Tigris River in the old land of Asshur. Nineveh is today called Mosul.

When at the ruins of Nineveh, we were impressed by the huge gates to the ancient city as restored by the government of Iraq.

In about 700 B.C. the Assyrians invaded the northern kingdom of Israel, and of the ten tribes that were not killed, they carried most into captivity to Nineveh. To this day, the fate of the Israelites taken to Assyria remains a mystery. According to inscriptions on the ruins of Sennacherib's palace in Nineveh, they must have been treated cruelly, and it is probable that most died in captivity.

When the Assyrian army besieged Jerusalem, King Hezekiah and the people turned to God and prayed for deliverance. According to 2 Kings 19:35-37, God intervened and one hundred eighty-five thousand Assyrian soldiers died outside the walls of Jerusalem. As a result, Sennacherib was forced to return to Nineveh. Afterward, two of his sons assassinated him, and another of his sons became king.

During the time of the Assyrian kingdom, Babylon was a province. We read in 2 Kings 17:24 that Babylonians were among those foreign races that Assyria brought into Israel to replace the Israelites taken into captivity. But soon after the defeat of the Assyrian army at Jerusalem, Babylon began to take a more prominent role in the Middle East. A delegation from Babylon came to Jerusalem to visit Hezekiah. The account of their visit is recorded in 2 Kings 20:14-19, *"Then came Isaiah the prophet unto king Hezekiah, and said unto him, What said these men? and from whence came they unto thee? And Hezekiah said, They are come from a far country, even from Babylon. And he said, What have they seen in thine house? And Hezekiah answered, All the things that are in mine house have they seen: there is nothing among my treasures that I have not shewed them. And Isaiah said unto Hezekiah, Hear the word of the Lord. Behold, the days come, that all that is in thine house, and that which thy fathers have laid up in store unto this day, shall be carried into Babylon: nothing shall be left, saith the Lord. And of thy sons that shall issue from thee, which thou shalt beget, shall they take away; and they shall be eunuchs in the palace of the king of Babylon. Then said Hezekiah unto Isaiah, Good is the word of the Lord which thou hast spoken. And he said, Is it not good, if peace and truth be in my days?"*

Although in the time of Isaiah Babylon was still only a province in the Assyrian kingdom, the prophet warns Israel to be on guard against it, and in seven chapters of Isaiah, God's sure judgment against this city is pronounced. For example, we read in Isaiah 21:9, *". . . Babylon is fallen, is fallen; and all the graven images of her gods he hath broken unto the ground."*

Concerning the decline of Assyria and the rise of Babylon, we quote from *A History Of the Middle East* by Sidney Fisher:

> *"One of the great empires controlling a major part of the Middle East was that of the Assyrians, whose capital was at Nineveh on the upper Tigris in Mesopotamia. Iron weapons, a*

disciplined army, a tight bureaucracy, and iron battering rams mounted on wheels gave the Semitic Assyrians such an advantage in the seventh century B.C. that Nineveh held sway from Sinai to the Caspian Sea and from the Persian Gulf to the plains of central Asia Minor. However, over-extension of the empire and exhausting battles, coupled with luxury, indolence, and unwise taxation, weakened the army and the government so that Nineveh and its palaces and great library were sacked by Iranians in league with another Semitic group which established its capital at Babylon on the Euphrates. Comprising the full Fertile Crescent from Sinai to the Persian Gulf, the new Chaldean Empire won fame from the 'hanging gardens,' from the Babylonian captivity of the Hebrews, and from such names as Nebuchad-nezzar and Belshazzar."

Nebuchadnezzar became king of Babylon in 606 B.C. His first two objectives were to build Babylon into the strongest and most magnificent city on earth, and to conquer all the world. According to 2 Kings 24-25, Judah became a province of Babylon, and Nebuchad-nezzar made three separate agreements with Jehoakim, Jehoiachin, and Zedekiah. On two separate occasions, he sent his army against Jerusalem to enforce his rule, and finally Nebuchadnezzar himself led his army against the city, sacked it, burned the Temple, and carried many of the holy vessels back to Babylon.

Although successful in escaping from Jerusalem, Zedekiah was captured at Jericho. Zedekiah's sons were killed before his eyes, and then he was blinded, leaving him with this terrible memory of the last thing he saw. All of the men of the royal line of David who were not killed were, like Daniel, made eunuchs. This was another attempt by Satan to prevent the birth of the Messiah.

The name of the first Babylon — Babel — means confusion. The name of the first ruler — Nimrod — comes from the word *marad*, which means "he rebelled." Such kings mark the entire course of Babylon's history — confusing the people and rebelling against God.

Therefore, it is no small wonder that Saddam Hussein, the present dictator of Iraq, has been described as the most arrogant and dangerous man in the world.

Chapter Three

Babylon's Fall and Decline

Babylon, before Nebuchadnezzar, was built on the west side of the Euphrates. But Nebuchadnezzar almost doubled its size by building a new city on the east bank. The overall size after the addition was fifteen miles square; therefore, we see Babylon again as one of Satan's many counterfeit schemes to deceive the world, because the New Jerusalem will be fifteen hundred miles square.

Babylon could raise an army of two hundred thousand, so it is concluded that the total population was about one million. Around the city was a wall three hundred fifty feet high and eighty-seven feet thick. Outside the inner wall, equally high, was a second wall. The second wall was one-half mile distant from the first wall, and between the two walls there was thirty square miles of fertile soil. In this area fruit trees of every kind bore fruit practically the year round, and the land could also be used to grow vegetables in times of siege. The Euphrates River ran through Babylon, and water was diverted to fill a thirty-foot wide moat outside the wall to further discourage invaders. With the morning and evening sun, the reflection off the polished bronze gates gave the wide avenues a golden appearance; so in every respect (size, river, and fruit trees) the city was designed to look like the New Jerusalem.

Nebuchadnezzar died in 561 B.C. Three male members of his family sat upon the throne in succession over a period of six years; all were assassinated. Finally, an in-law, Nabonnedus, a military strong man, took the throne in 555 B.C. But Nabonnedus was a general, and the empire was being challenged from the east, the west, and the south. And so King Nabonnedus invested most of his time fighting enemies out in the provinces while the second and third ruler of the kingdom sat on the throne. For some unknown reason, Nabonnedus spent several years at an oasis in northwest Arabia. Receiving word that the Medes and Persians were besieging Babylon, he led his army to Haran in Syria, his mother's birthplace. A Haranian inscription, found by archaeologists, records Nabonnedus as saying:

> *"But I hide myself afar from my city of Babylon . . . ten years to my city Babylon I went not in."*

In 547 B.C., the Medes and Persians crossed the Tigris and began an assault upon the provinces of Babylon, and actually conquered and held much of the territory including Haran. And so, according to a dream Nabonnedus had, as found in the ruins of Haran, he engaged the enemy in Syria rather than returning to help defend Babylon. The dream is as follows:

> *"At the beginning of my reign the gods let*

> *me see a dream: in it there stood both Marduk,*
> *the Great Lord, and Sin, the light of heaven*
> *and earth. Marduk said to me: 'Nabonnedus,*
> *King of Babylon, bring bricks on your own*
> *horse and chariot and build the temple of*
> *Elulhul* [the moon god] *that Sin, the Great*
> *Lord, may take up his dwelling there.' I replied*
> *to Marduk, the chief of the gods, 'Barbarian*
> *hordes* [the Medes], *are laying siege to the very*
> *temple you have ordered me to build and their*
> *armed might is very great.' But Marduk said to*
> *me, 'The barbarians of whom you spoke, they,*
> *and their country, and all the kings who march*
> *at their side, shall cease to exist'* . . . *That was*
> *the doing of the Great Lord Marduk, whose*
> *command cannot be changed."*

Nabonnedus was, evidently, given a temporary victory at Haran and did build a temple to Marduk. The temple of Marduk (the same as the Canaanite god Baal) at Babylon has been restored. But the victory over the Medes at Haran was a rather insignificant one as it in no way affected the final outcome of the war. All these ancient writings of Nabonnedus prove that the Book of Daniel is correct — at the time that Belshazzar, Nabonnedus' son (or adopted son), was on the throne, the nation had renounced the God of Daniel and returned to worshipping the false gods and idols of the Babylonians.

According to the book *Babylon* by John Oates,

during the reigns of Nabonnedus and Belshazzar, inflation amounted to two hundred percent. The population resented the return to religious oppression and fanaticism. Taxes were increased to support army expenditures and to build the temples of Marduk and Sin. There was a revival of idol worship that existed in the early days of Nebuchadnezzar.

It seems the majority of the people, according to both Grecian and Persian accounts, were overburdened, discouraged, and disillusioned. The setting for Daniel 5:1-4 is the year 539 B.C. while Nabonnedus and the bulk of the Babylonian army was at Haran:

> *"Belshazzar the king made a great feast to a thousand of his lords, and drank wine before the thousand. Belshazzar, whiles he tasted the wine, commanded to bring the golden and silver vessels which his father Nebuchadnezzar had taken out of the temple which was in Jerusalem; that the king, and his princes, his wives, and his concubines, might drink therein. . . . They drank wine, and praised the gods of gold, and of silver, of brass, of iron, of wood, and of stone."*

The occasion for this gala event ordered by Belshazzar was the New Year Festival. Again quoting from *Babylon* by John Oates:

> *"In 539 B.C. the New Year Festival was*

> *celebrated in Babylon, apparently for the first time since Nabonnedus' retirement in Taima; the Persian account ascribes to the Babylonian king various sacreligious actions during the festival. During the ceremony a plentiful supply of wine was distributed, and to judge from the accounts of Herodotus, Xenophon, and the author of the Book of Daniel, not only were the revels prolonged, but the memory of them remained fresh for many years."*

We also quote from the book *Babylonia and Syria* by H.W.F. Saggs:

> *"During the first five days of the festival, various ceremonies of purification and preparation were performed. These culminated in the High Priest taking the King in before Marduk, to whom he surrendered his royal insignia. . . . On the sixth day the image of the god Nabu arrived . . . and entered the temple of his father Marduk. The details of what Marduk and Nabu did during the following days we do not know: in general terms it is likely that they were engaged in decreeing the fate of the city for the following year. . . . The climax of the festival took place on the tenth day. The statues of Marduk, Nabu, and other gods, dressed in sacred garments adorned in gold, assembled in the great courtyard. . . . After*

*his victory Marduk and his procession were
taken back to the city in triumph, the populace
shouting over and over again their ritual cries
of joy."*

During the New Year Festival in Babylon, the king
and his court were celebrating with wine as was the usual
custom. However, this year they drank to their false
gods from the sacred vessels of the temple. It was their
way of showing contempt for the God of Daniel.

The city was under siege and facing an uncertain
future, so Belshazzar was looking forward to the gods of
Babylon to make known the fate of the city. However,
the prophecy concerning the future came not from
Babylon's gods, but the God of the Hebrews. A finger
appeared in the air and wrote on the wall, *"Mene, Mene,
Tekel, Upharsin."* We can readily understand why the
king became deathly afraid and his knees shook.

It was then that the queen suggested that Daniel be
brought in to interpret the writing. Daniel reminded
Belshazzar that his God had humbled Nebuchadnezzar
until he acknowledged Him as the Most High who ruled
in the kingdom of men. Daniel also added: *"And thou
his son, O Belshazzar, hast not humbled thine heart,
though thou knewest all this; But hast lifted up thyself
against the Lord of heaven; and they have brought the
vessels of his house before thee, and thou, and thy lords,
thy wives, and thy concubines, have drunk wine in them;
and thou hast praised the gods of silver, and gold, of
brass, iron, wood, and stone, which see not, nor hear,*

nor know: and the God in whose hand thy breath is, and whose are all thy ways, hast thou not glorified" (Dan. 5:22-23).

Daniel then told Belshazzar the interpretation of the writing on the wall concerning the future of the city, *"God hath numbered thy kingdom, and finished it . . . Thou art weighed in the balances, and art found wanting . . . Thy kingdom is divided, and given to the Medes and Persians"* (Dan. 5:26-28).

And we read in verses thirty and thirty-one: *"In that night was Belshazzar the king of the Chaldeans slain. And Darius the Median took the kingdom. . . ."*

Nabonnedus did march with his army from the east, but it was too late. He was defeated between the Tigris and Euphrates, and his army annihilated. According to Herodotus, the Medes and the Persians diverted the river into a depression near Aqar Quf; the moat around the city was drained, and they marched into Babylon during the festival unopposed. The historian stated:

> *"As it was, the Persians came upon them by surprise and so took the city. Owing to the vast size of the place, the inhabitants of the central parts, as the residents of Babylon declare, long after the outer portions of the town were taken, knew nothing of what had chanced, but as they were engaged in a festival, continued dancing and revelling until they learnt the capture but too certainly."*

According to archaeological evidence in the book

Babylonia and Assyria, because of discontent and religious oppression in Babylon under Belshazzar, the Medes and Persians had Babylonian traitors inside the city, who worked from within, to help them swiftly take the city without a fight. Babylon itself suffered no destruction. History and archaeology verify the biblical account of the fall of Babylon to the Medes and the Persians in every detail.

The New Year Festival in Babylon celebrated by Belshazzar occurred when the sun crossed the vernal equinox in the spring. The fesival of Babylon in 1987 began when the sun crossed the vernal equinox in the fall on September 22. The stated reason for this festival is to prove that God is wrong and that Babylon has risen once more from the sands of time to erase the writing on the wall that appeared twenty-five hundred years ago.

According to both the biblical and historical records, the change of government in Babylon was an easy one for the Medes and Persians. Most Babylonians actually welcomed the conquerers as deliverers. Taxes were lightened and trade and commerce thrived. The Jews were given their freedom and many returned to rebuild Jerusalem and the Temple.

When the Persian King Xerxes launched his war against Greece, many of his troops and supplies were provided by Babylon. However, when he attempted to place a heavier burden on Babylon for the war effort, the Babylonians rebelled and threw the Persians out. But Xerxes besieged the city, overthrew the rebels, and burned the temple of Marduk. However, the fortunes of

Babylon turned once more. Quoting from *Babylon* by John Oates:

> *"In 465 B.C. Xerxes was assassinated and succeeded by his younger son, Artaxerxes, who seems to have held a more sympathetic attitude toward Babylon. To the priests of Marduk he restored their lands and their positions, but it is doubtful whether much of their temple was standing at this time. However, the detailed descriptions of Herodotus show that despite its harsh treatment, the city was far from destroyed."*

In 332 B.C. Alexander the Great set out from Macedonia with the intent of defeating the Persian Empire and then conquering the world. His strategy was to first take all the cities from Constantinople to Alexandria to deprive the Persian fleet of its bases. At Assissi on the Mediterranean coast, in what is now southern Turkey, he learned of a trap that had been set for him by the Persians. In a daring maneuver, he marched inland and caught the Persians in their own trap. He then marched southward past Tyre and Sidon to the mouth of the Nile, and doubled back. He made Babylon his eastern capital and took all the land as far as India. In India he met with disaster and lost over half of his army in retreating back to Babylon, where he became ill and died in 323 B.C.

Under the divided Grecian Empire, Antiochus

Seleucus established a nearby city with his own name and forced the population of Babylon to move there. Later, Antiochus Epiphanes in 173 B.C. repopulated the city with a small Grecian population, but it did not last. In 24 B.C. Strabo described Babylon as being most empty and desolate. The Jewish population of the area that remained continued to maintain Babylon's identity in a town on the outskirts with a population of fifteen thousand. The Apostle Peter was commissioned by Jesus Christ to take the gospel to the Jews, and in 63 A.D. he concluded his first epistle with these words: *"The church that is at Babylon, elected together with you, saluteth you; and so doth Marcus my son"* (1 Pet. 5:13). Some interpret Babylon to be Rome, but had Peter been in Rome, there is no reason why he should not have said so. Beyond doubt, the apostle was in Babylon.

In 116 A.D. the Roman General Trajan wintered in Babylon during his war against the Parthians, but he reported that the city itself was mostly desolate and empty. Before departing, he offered a sacrifice in the room where Alexander died. In succeeding centuries, the Euphrates River changed its course and buried the city of Nebuchadnezzar under sand before changing its course once more. There ancient Babylon slept until 1899, the beginning of the twentieth century, when Robert Koldewey on behalf of Germany, began excavations and unearthed the upper portions of the Ishtar Gate.

Of the coming of Israel's Messiah to establish His kingdom and rebuild the nation of Israel, we read in

Isaiah 48:12, 14, 20: *"Hearken unto me, O Jacob and Israel, my called; I am he; I am the first, I also am the last . . . All ye, assemble yourselves, and hear; which among them hath declared these things? The Lord hath loved him: he will do his pleasure on Babylon, and his arms shall be on the Chaldeans . . . Go ye forth of Babylon, flee ye from the Chaldeans, with a voice of singing declare ye, tell this, utter it even to the end of the earth; say ye, The Lord hath redeemed his servant Jacob.*

The government of Iraq says that Babylon will live again and defy the judgment of God. But the Bible says that God will do his pleasure on Babylon, and it will be destroyed in one day, never to rise again.

Chapter Four

Babylon the Harlot

There are well-meaning and even knowledgeable Bible scholars who contend that all the prophecies relating to Babylon, even those in Revelation, were fulfilled in the Persian, Macedonian, and Hellenistic periods, before the birth of Jesus Christ. But Babylon was not destroyed in a day; it was not wiped off the face of the earth in a fiery judgment within an hour's time; its name is still remembered; and there were no martyrs of Jesus who died in old Babylon. Therefore, we have to look elsewhere, other than the Babylon that Nebuchadnezzar built, for the identity of mystery Babylon of the last days.

We first read Revelation 17:1-7, *"And there came one of the seven angels which had the seven vials, and talked with me, saying unto me, Come hither; I will shew unto thee the judgment of the great whore that sitteth upon many waters: With whom the kings of the earth have committed fornication, and the inhabitants of the earth have been made drunk with the wine of her fornication. So he carried me away in the spirit into the wilderness: and I saw a woman sit upon a scarlet coloured beast, full of names of blasphemy, having seven heads and ten horns. And the woman was arrayed in purple and scarlet colour, and decked with gold and precious stones and pearls, having a golden cup in her hand full of abominations and filthiness of her fornication: And upon her forehead was a name written, MYSTERY, BABYLON THE GREAT, THE MOTHER OF HARLOTS AND ABOMINATIONS OF THE EARTH. And I saw the woman drunken with the blood of the saints, and with the blood of the martyrs of Jesus: and when I saw her, I wondered with great admiration. And the angel said unto me, Wherefore didst thou marvel? I will tell thee the mystery of the woman, and of the beast that carrieth her, which hath the seven heads and ten horns."*

It is generally agreed by all reputable Bible scholars who have offered a commentary on Revelation 17 that Babylon, the "mother of harlots," is an evil religious system. This conclusion follows the symbolism set forth in Scripture. The church, the bride of Christ, is referred to as a chaste virgin. Jezebel, the wife of Ahab, was a prime example of degenerate womanhood, and we read in Revelation 2:20, *"Notwithstanding I have a few things against thee, because thou sufferest that woman Jezebel, which calleth herself a prophetess, to teach and to seduce my servants to commit fornication, and to eat things sacrificed unto idols."*

We notice that the woman is arrayed in purple. Purple is the color of royalty, so the symbolism follows that she is the concubine of kings. She is also adorned in scarlet, and the color of scarlet on a woman is traditionally the identification color of prostitutes. The harlot has evidently been rewarded for her services because she is also decked with gold, precious stones, pearls, and has a golden cup in her hand. If you have ever been to the huge cathedrals in Europe, like the ones at Toledo in Spain, the comparative symbolism is strking. In these cathedrals there are billions of dollars worth of gold ornaments and images, and jewels beyond imagination.

Now we notice that the harlot comes riding upon a scarlet colored beast. Predatory beasts in the Bible are used as symbols of empires, and they still are today — the lion, bear, leopard, etc. The symbolism is again apparent. The political system or the alliance that will ultimately produce the Antichrist will allow the religious system to ride along for the support and pleasure the beast receives. The harlot will play her part in deceiving all the unsaved world to worship the Antichrist as god.

In Revelation 17:7 we notice again the words of the angel: *". . . I will tell thee the mystery of the woman, and of the beast that carrieth her. . . ."* After the angel described the political beast, he spoke again to John: *"And he saith unto me, The waters which thou sawest, where the whore sitteth, are peoples, and multitudes, and nations, and tongues. And the ten horns which thou sawest upon the beast, these shall hate the whore, and shall make her desolate and naked, and shall eat her flesh, and burn her with fire. For God hath put in their hearts to fulfil his will, and to agree, and give their kingdom unto the beast, until the words of God shall be fulfilled. And the woman which thou sawest is that great city, which reigneth over the kings of the earth"* (Rev. 17:15-18).

There is a jingle which goes:

> There was a young lady of Niger,
> Who smiled as she rode on a tiger;
> They returned from the ride
> With the lady inside,
> And the smile on the face of the tiger.

This little rhyme illustrates the relation of the religious system to the kingdom of Antichrist during the tribulation period. The system of religion is destroyed by the Antichrist once she has served her purpose. Some believe the city to be Rome of the first century and the religious system that sprang from Rome. However, this is a conclusion and not a prophetic certainty. So there is still a mystery concerning the real identity of both the religious system and the kingdom of ten rulers. But the setting of the prophecy is the Great Tribulation, and during this period of seven years that precedes the coming of Jesus Christ to establish His kingdom on earth, the identity of both the woman and the beast may not be a mystery.

The city of the religious system of Revelation 17 becomes Babylon in Revelation 18. To understand the mystery religion of Babylon, we should first understand that all the gods of the Chaldeans sprang from the legend of Nimrod. In *The Two Babylons,* Alexander Hislop wrote in great detail concerning the evolvement of the religion of Babylon through the founder of Babel. Concerning some of these gods and goddesses we quote from the book *Babylon* by John Oates:

> "*The roots of Babylonian religion lie far back in the prehistoric past. Anu . . . who appears as a shadowy figure throughout Mesopotamian history, originally stood at its head. . . . Under various names Ishtar was later to become the most important goddess through Western Asia. . . . In late Babylonian times the title* Bel, Lord, *became synonymous with Marduk, who like Ishtar assimilated to himself various aspects of other gods. A second group of gods consisted of the astral deities, the Sun, the Moon, and the planet Venus. Of these the moon-god Sin was perhaps the most important. . . . Ishtar, goddess of love and war, was, like Shamash, a child of the moon-god. She was Venus, the Morning and Evening Star, and she often was represented riding on her sacred beast, the lion. . . . Closely associated with Ishtar, but whose rank in the pantheon is obscure, is Tammuz . . . whose death and disappearance it was custom to mourn. Much has been written about Tammuz and the mythology associated with his name on the assumption that he underwent an annual resurrection.*"

Another principal Babylonian god was Sin, the sun god, whose worship was often accompanied with the lighting of candles. There were many other gods in the Babylonian pantheon, and the religion of Babylon included amulets to ward off evil spirits and sacrifices to the demons. Marduk was the same as Baal of the Canaanites, and Ishtar was the Diana of the Ephesians and the Grecian world. All the gods of Babylon can be traced to the idols and gods of Greece, Rome, Egypt, and the heathen world. Hinduism and Buddhism are much like, in part, the mystery religion of Babylon.

After Nimrod died, according to the Babylonian tradition, his wife Semiramis bore a son whom she named Tammuz. She claimed that Tammuz was Nimrod reborn, the son of the sun god. This was a satanic deception of the promise of a coming Savior in Genesis 3:15: *"And I will put enmity between thee and the woman, and between thy seed and her seed; it shall bruise thy head, and thou shalt bruise his heel."* The resurrection of Tammuz was, of course, another part of the satanic lie. Semiramis claimed that her son was supernaturally conceived, so the mother was worshipped as well as the child. Many of the Jews in Babylon accepted, at least in part, this satanic religion, and one of the Jewish months is Tammuz. We read in Ezekiel 8:14-15, *"Then he brought me to the door of the gate of the Lord's house which was toward the north; and behold, there sat women weeping for Tammuz. Then said he unto me, Hast thou seen this, O son of man? turn thee yet again, and thou shalt see greater abominations than these."*

Concerning the spread of the mystery religion of Babylon, we quote from the book *Babylon Mystery Religion* by Ralph Woodrow:

> "*The Chinese had a mother goddess called Shingmoo or the 'Holy Mother.' She is pictured with child in arms and rays of glory around her head. The ancient Germans worshipped the virgin Hertha with child in arms. The Scandinavians called her Disa, who was also pictured with child. The Etruscans called her Nutria and among the Druids the Virgo-Patitura was worshipped as the 'Mother of God.' In India, she was known as Indrani, who also was represented with child in arms. The mother goddess was known as Aphrodite to the Greeks; Nana, to the Sumerians; and as Venus to her devotees in the olden days of Rome, and her child was Jupiter. . . . In Asia, the mother was known as Cybele and the child as Deoius.*
>
> " '*But regardless of her name or place,' says one writer, 'she was the wife of Baal, the virgin queen of heaven, who bore fruit although she never conceived.' When the children of Israel fell into apostasy, they too were defiled with this mother goddess worship. As we read in Judges 2:13: 'They forsook the Lord, and served Baal and Ashtaroth.'*
>
> "*. . . One of the titles by which the goddess was known among them was 'the queen of*

heaven' (Jer. 44:17-19). . . . The prophet Jeremiah rebuked them for worshipping her. . . . In Ephesus, the great mother was known as Diana. The temple dedicated to her in that city was one of the seven wonders of the ancient world! Not only at Ephesus, but throughout all Asia and the world was the goddess worshipped (Acts 19:27). In Egypt, the mother was known as Isis and her child as Horus. . . . This false worship, having spread from Babylon to the various nations, in different names and forms, finally became established at Rome and throughout the Roman Empire."

It should also be noted that many of the idols of Diana by the idol makers at Ephesus were made with a replica of the Tower of Babel on top of her head, recognizing the false religion of Babylon and that the goddess was actually the wife of Nimrod. The worship of the pseudo-goddess and her offspring in all nations can be traced back to Babel and the incorporation of this satanic deception into the mystery religion of Babylon. Israel and Judah were warned repeatedly by the prophets of God to reject this prostitution by the devil of the promise of a coming Redeemer, but they continued to follow the false prophets of Baal such as Jezebel. Finally, God allowed them first to be subjugated by Assyria and then by Babylon from whence the religion came.

Isaiah repeatedly warned Israel against worshipping

the gods and goddesses of Babylon, but then the prophet pointed to the birth of the true Savior of God: *". . . Hear ye now, O house of David; Is it a small thing for you to weary men, but will ye weary my God also? Therefore the Lord himself shall give you a sign; Behold, a virgin shall conceive, and bear a son, and shall call his name Immanuel"* (Isa. 7:13-14).

In the fullness of time a virgin by the name of Mary did conceive and bear a Son by the Holy Ghost. Certainly Mary was a handmaiden of the Lord, especially chosen according to time, circumstances, and heritage to bring the Savior into the world to save sinners. She is to be called blessed by all who receive Jesus Christ as Lord and Savior. But there is no scripture in all the Bible that even implies that her birth was of a divine nature, that she was sinless, that she was caught up to Heaven, or that she is to be worshipped or prayed to by Christians. None of the apostles or disciples worshipped her or directed intercessions before God to her. There is not one single word of evidence in the records of the early church that Mary was worshipped or considered more than being the mother of the Lord. *"For there is one God, and one mediator between God and men, the man Christ Jesus; Who gave himself a ransom for all, to be testified in due time"* (1 Tim. 2:5-6).

The *Encyclopaedia Britannica* states that in the Christian churches of the first centuries, no emphasis was placed upon the worship of Mary. The *Catholic Encyclopedia* reports:

*"Devotion to our Blessed Lady in its
ultimate analysis must be regarded as a practical
application of the doctrine of the Communion
of Saints. Seeing that this doctrine is not
contained, at least explicitly, in the earlier
forms of the Apostles' Creed, there is perhaps
no ground for surprise if we do not meet with
any clear traces of the cultus of the Blessed
Virgin in the first Christian centuries."*

It was not until the Emperor Constantine made
Christianity the state religion of the Roman Empire that
Marilogy became an important part of church doctrine.
Because of the Babylonish religion that had spread to all
the world, it became easier for the heathen world to
profess allegiance to the state church if the main beliefs
in the traditions of Nimrod could be incorporated into
worship. In 431 A.D. at the Council of Ephesus, the
worship of Mary in the form that is prevalent today was
adopted as an official church doctrine.

In the book *Babylon Mystery Religion*, the author
states:

*"A further indication that Mary worship
developed out of the old worship of the mother
goddess may be seen in the tiles by which the
Babylonian goddess was known. In deified
form, Nimrod came to be known as Baal. The
title of his wife, the female divinity, would be in
the equivalent of Baalti. In English, the word*

*means, 'My Lady'; in Latin, 'Mea Domina';
and in Italian, it is corrupted into the well-
known 'Madonna'!"*

Therefore, it is no mystery that the government of
Iraq has stated that the rock star Madonna of the United
States lives in the heart of the Iraqi people, and why she
was invited to reign as queen over the Festival of
Babylon in 1987.

Chapter Five

Babylon In the Church

In our previous chapter we discussed the attempt by Satan to counterfeit the promise of God to send the seed of woman to bruise the serpent's head. This deception came first before the flood when Satan attempted to defile the entire human race through fallen angelic corruption. After the flood, Satan diverted the attention of mankind from the coming Savior through the rise of a false religion, Mystery Babylon. As we have already noted, the base of this satanic counterfeit salvation was the myth that after Nimrod's death his wife gave birth to a son whom she named Tammuz. The worship of Nimrod's wife, Semiramis, as the queen of heaven and her god-son spread throughout the world. It exists today in many forms, even within Christendom.

A tradition related to the religion of Babylon is that when Nimrod died, his body was cut into pieces, cremated, and the ashes were spread over the earth. In Judges 19 we find what may be considered a comparative story about a concubine who went out from her master and became a whore. Her flesh and bones were cut into many pieces and scattered throughout the coasts of Israel. The origin of such heathenish practices was probably in the scattering of Nimrod's human parts, and may illustrate the dissemination of the religion of Babylon into all the world.

In the case of Nimrod, according to the tradition as related by some ancient sources, all of the body was cut up and scattered with the exception of his reproductive organs. It was from this ancient and obscure Babylonian tradition that the worship of the "phallus" began.

In Genesis 10 we read that Ham begat Cush, and Cush begat Nimrod. It is generally agreed by most Bible scholars that Nimrod was a black man. The next great king of Babylon to arise after Nimrod was Hammurabi, his name signifying that he was a descendant of Nimrod through Ham. The laws of Hammurabi were graven on a large black stone in the shape of a phallus.

It Egypt Semiramis took the name of Isis, and Tammuz became Horus. The *Encyclopedia Of Religions* (Vol. 3, p. 264) states that Queen Semiramis in Babylon erected an obelisk one hundred thirty feet high to the memory of Nimrod. Such temples were common in Babylon and later in Egypt. These obelisks are replete in the temples of Luxor and Karnak. Many of the monuments have been removed to other nations. One stands in Central Park in New York City, one in London, and others in Italy.

According to *The Two Babylons* by Hislop and *Babylon Mystery Religion* by Woodrow, these obelisks, or standing images as they were called in the Hebrew, are mentioned in both 1 Kings and 2 Kings as a part of Baal worship. Baal is one of the names for Nimrod. It was into this kind of evil and licentious religion that Jezebel enticed Israel. It is to the abolition of the last vestiges of the Babylonian idolatry that Isaiah 27:1 and 9 is addressed, *"In that day the Lord with his sore and great and strong sword shall punish leviathan the piercing serpent, even leviathan that crooked serpent; and he shall slay the dragon that is in the sea . . . By this therefore shall the iniquity of Jacob be purged; and this is all the fruit to take away his sin; when he maketh all the stones of the altar as chalkstones that are beaten in sunder, the groves and images shall not stand up."*

A common practice in Egypt, Greece, and other nations of the Middle East and the Mediterranean area, where the religion of Babylon had spread was to erect an obelisk in front of the temple. This symbolism for the phallus associated the religion with the fertility cult of Nimrod. The temples of Diana, the Ephesian counterpart of Nimrod's wife, the queen of heaven, was supported by the temple prostitutes. According to Ezekiel 8:1-6, this abominable symbol was erected in front of the temple at the north gate. Ezekiel referred to it as the "image of jealousy." We can be certain that it was the Babylonian symbol of Nimrod because we read in verse fourteen that the prophet saw a woman at the temple weeping for Tammuz, the son of Nimrod.

Emperor Caligula was one of the most cruel and degenerate of the Caesars of Rome. According to the book *Babylon Mystery Religion*, Caligula transported an obelisk from Heliopolis in Egypt to the section of Rome which was called his *circus*. This hill is the place where the Vatican was later built. The obelisk remained in the Vatican until 1586 when Pope Sixtus V had it moved in front of the church at St. Peter where it is today. The pope had decreed the death penalty if it should be broken or damaged. The mover was a man named Domenico Fontana. Forty-five winches, one hundred sixty horses, and a crew of eight hundred men were required to move the obelisk to its new location. When the task was completed, the pope blessed it and the workmen who had moved it under such an extreme penalty for failure. An inscription in the pagan temple of Heliopolis, from where the obelisk came, reads: *"I, Dionysus, dedicated these phalli to Hera, my step-mother."* The account of the moving of the obelisk can be found in the Hasting's *Encyclopedia Of Religion and Ethics* in a section on "phallicism."

It is also interesting to take note that the obelisk in front of St. Peter's Cathedral came from Heliopolis. We read in Jeremiah 43:13, *"He shall break also the images of Beth-shemesh, that is in the land of Egypt; and the houses of the gods of the Egyptians shall he burn with fire."* The footnote in the Pilgrim Bible on Beth-shemesh reads, *"This means 'House of the Sun,' or temples dedicated to sun-worship. . . . This was probably the city which was called Heliopolis by the Greeks."*

Wherever we have gone in the world, we have seen the obelisk in its relationship to the mystery religion of Babylon. In Egypt we saw them at the temples of Luxor and Karnak. In China we saw the entire land punctuated with Buddhist shrines called *pagodas*. These pagodas rise high in the sky in tiers, much like the Tower of Babel, and the phallus symbol of Nimrod. In China Semiramis, the mother goddess, was called Shingmoo. Throughout the Moslem world from Morocco, to Egypt, to Syria, Jordan, and Iraq we have seen mosques surrounded by minarets, slender spires with an enlarged section at the top. The symbolism is apparent. Mecca, in the heart of Islam, fractures the skyline with a host of minarets with their slight enlargements at the apex.

In the fourth and fifth centuries, the Roman Empire divided into two parts, with Constantinople becoming the capital city of the eastern leg. The church at St. Sophia was the pride of the holy Byzantine Empire. In front of St. Sophia in the town square was erected a tall obelisk. This obelisk is still standing today. When we were in Istanbul, our guide informed us that it was at this obelisk where doctrinal disagreements were settled through athletic contests. After the Turks captured Constantinople in 1292 and changed the name to Istanbul, St. Sophia was converted to a mosque and minarets were erected around it.

In temples, shrines, mosques, and churches of all religions of the world, obelisk-like spires and towers are included in construction. Many of these elongated units simply follow tradition without any realization of their meaning or relationship to the mystery religion of Babylon.

The obelisk in front of St. Peter's in Rome, including the foundation, is one hundred thirty-two feet high. Inasmuch as it came from Heliopolis in Egypt, it is probably no coincidence that it is approximately the same height as the one that Queen Semiramis erected in honor of her husband, Nimrod. But the largest obelisk in the world is in front of our nation's capitol building in Washington, D.C., the Washington Monument. Again, it was probably no coincidence that the phallus-shaped obelisk was chosen to memorialize George Washington as the father of the United States. We will comment on its relationship to Mystery Babylon later in this study.

As we consider the major religions of mankind, there are literally hundreds of connections that could be made to the mystery religion of Babylon. The most prominent, besides the obelisk, is the worship of idols, or the use of idols in worship.

As evil as the thoughts and deeds of mankind became in the millennium before the flood, there is no evidence that idol worship was among its sins. Idol worship originated at Babel, and after Babel, as the people were scattered over the face of the earth, they carried with them this religious abomination. Throughout Egypt, the Hebrews were confronted with idols to the Egyptian gods, which in reality were only Babylonian gods that had been given Egyptian names. When they passed through the lands of the Canaanite tribes, they saw similar idols which had been given Canaanite names. Therefore, the Lord gave this commandment to Moses for the Israelites: "*Ye shall make you no idols nor graven image, neither rear you up a standing image, neither shall ye set up any image of stone in your land, to bow down unto it: for I am the Lord your God*" (Lev. 26:1).

The Babylonian concept of idol worship was the chief weapon of Satan that the prophets of God had to contend with. There are thousands of references in the Old Testament alone to idol worship. Like a large segment of both Catholic and non-Catholic Christendom today, the Hebrews tried to make a pretense of worshipping God while catering to their idolatry. We read in Jeremiah 7:8-10, 18, 30-31: *"Behold, ye trust in lying words, that cannot profit. Will ye steal, murder, and commit adultery, and swear falsely, and burn incense unto Baal, and walk after other gods whom ye know not; And come and stand before me in this house, which is called by my name, and say, We are delivered to do all these abominations? . . . The children gather wood, and the fathers kindle the fire, and the women knead their dough, to make cakes to the queen of heaven, and to pour out drink offerings unto other gods . . . For the children of Judah have done evil in my sight, saith the Lord: they have set their abominations in the house which is called by my name, to pollute it. And they have built the high places of Tophet, which is in the valley of the son of Hinnom, to burn their sons and their daughters in the fire; which I commanded them not. . . ."*

It was the worship of idols, mainly Baal (Nimrod) and the queen of heaven (Nimrod's wife) that brought the judgment of God upon the nation. In the early church it was idol worshippers and makers at Ephesus and other cities who were the fiercest enemies of the disciples. In Athens, the city was overrun with idols, so much so that they even had an idol to the unknown god!

In Rome, at the Pantheon, there were idols to every god in the known world.

Like the Israelites, there were some in the early church who professed Jesus Christ as Lord and Savior, yet clung to their heathen idols. We read of this abomination in 2 Corinthians 6:15-17, *"And what concord hath Christ with Belial? or what part hath he that believeth with an infidel? And what agreement hath the temple of God with idols? . . . Wherefore come out from among them, and be ye separate, saith the Lord, and touch not the unclean thing; and I will receive you."*

In India the Hindu temples are filled with idols of the Babylonian fertility cult; in Bangkok the temples are likewise filled with idols; in China the Buddhist temples have the largest idols in the world. After the Council of Ephesus in 431 A.D. sanctioned the worship of the god-mother religion, the churches of Asia became filled with idols. When Mohammed ravaged the churches of this territory early in the seventh century, he brought fifteen hundred idols back to Mecca. Regardless how identifiable statues are with Christianity, it is an abomination to worship and kiss them. We read in 1 Kings 19:18, *". . . I have left me seven thousand in Israel, all the knees which have not bowed unto Baal, and every mouth which hath not kissed him."* Kissing an idol is associated with the worship of Baal, or Nimrod.

All idol worship is related to the mystery religion of Babylon, and all religions are invested with it to some degree. The time is coming when the world religion of the tribulation, Mystery Babylon, will call upon all idol worshippers on earth to worship one idol, the image of Antichrist. *"And he had power to give life unto the image of the beast, that the image of the beast should both speak, and cause that as many as would not worship the image of the beast should be killed"* (Rev. 13:15).

The religion of Babel was centered in the person of Nimrod. This religion was to weld a one-world worship in rebellion against God. After Babel this fractured religion was carried into all the world where it has been propagated and perpetuated in various forms. However, its stronghold was retained in Babylon. It would appear that at the fall of Babylon God placed barriers upon this satanic deception and his fallen angels to prevent it from corrupting the entire world. But according to the prophetic Word of God, at the end of the age fractured Babylonianism would unite once more to produce another world leader who would defy God and declare to the whole world that he is god. This we see taking place today. We read in Revelation 9:13-15: *"And the sixth angel sounded, and I heard a voice from the four horns of the golden altar which is before God, Saying to the sixth angel which had the trumpet, Loose the four angels which are bound in the great river Euphrates. And the four angels were loosed, which were prepared for an hour, and a day, and a month, and a year, for to slay the third part of men."*

This prophetic warning is repeated in Revelation 16:12-14: *"And the sixth angel poured out his vial upon the great river Euphrates; and the water thereof was dried up, that the way of the kings of the east might be prepared. And I saw three unclean spirits like frogs come out of the mouth of the dragon, and out of the mouth of the beast, and out of the mouth of the false prophet. For they are the spirits of devils, working miracles, which go forth unto the kings of the earth and of the whole world, to gather them to the battle of that great day of God Almighty."*

The confusion within Christendom today, the rise of Eastern religions in our own nation, and the rapid growth of the New Age movement indicate that mankind is rapidly approaching the Great Tribulation and Jesus Christ will come as a thief for those who are not watching.

The major religions of mankind today are looking for a messiah to come. The New Age religion adherents are predicting that Maitreya will come; messianic fervor is now sweeping Israel; a large segment of the Islamic nations see in Saddam Hussein their Mahdi. This too is a sign that Jesus Christ, the true Messiah, may appear at any time (Matt. 24:23-27).

Chapter Six

The Babylonian Priesthood

As we continue our study of the Mystery Babylon of the last days, we take particular notice of the relationship of the religious system, called the Great Whore, to the political empire of Antichrist and the kings of the earth. We read in Revelation 14:8-10: *"And there followed another angel, saying, Babylon is fallen, is fallen, that great city, because she made all nations drink of the wine of the wrath of her fornication. And the third angel followed them, saying with a loud voice, If any man worship the beast and his image, and receive his mark in his forehead, or in his hand, The same shall drink of the wine of the wrath of God, which is poured out without mixture into the cup of his indignation; and he shall be tormented with fire and brimstone in the presence of the holy angels, and in the presence of the Lamb."*

In Revelation 17 the "mother of harlots" is depicted riding on the back of the political beast, and in Revelation 18:3 we read that the kings of the earth commit fornication with her.

Nimrod, the founder of Babylon, was not only the king of Babel, he was also a high priest. And from Nimrod came a priesthood that directed the worship of the people to the king of the empire as a god. The priesthood of Nimrod was carried on in various nations and religions in many forms and functions. In Buddhism and Hinduism, the prevalent religions of the East, a succession of priests to intercede between the people and the gods have continued to this day. In Egypt there was also a priesthood who served in the temples and worshipped Pharaoh as a god. In the early church there were those who attempted to establish the authority of such a priesthood over the churches, and it was these false priests to whom Revelation 2:6 is addressed: *"But this thou hast, that thou hatest the deeds of the Nicolaitanes, which I also hate."*

In the year 63 B.C., Julius Caesar was given the official title of "Pontifex Maximus," meaning the high priest. The Caesars were not only the high priests over the Babylonish religious system of the Roman Empire; they were, like Nimrod, hailed as gods. Like Nimrod, each was the high priest, god, and king. This was a satanic corruption of the position of Jesus Christ within the Godhead. As our High Priest, He is God, and He is King of kings. There is a Roman coin of the first century B.C. which shows Augustus Caesar with the title "Ponti-Max."

The priesthood of Israel, with the high priest at the head, was established by God through Aaron. All the offices within this priesthood, and its functions, were for the purpose of directing the worship of Israel to God, to intercede between them and God, and to offer up animal sacrifices for sin until the Messiah came and offered up one sacrifice for sin for all. If there is one nation, or one religion, on the face of the earth with reason to establish and carry on such a priesthood, it is Israel under Judaism today. But we find no such priesthood or high priest in Israel. Why? Because when Jesus Christ came and died on the cross, and the Temple was subsequently destroyed, that priesthood was abolished. We read in Hebrews 9:11-14, *"But Christ being come an high priest of good things to come, by a greater and more perfect tabernacle, not made with hands, that is to say, not of this building; Neither by the blood of goats and calves, but by his own blood he entered in once into the holy place, having obtained eternal redemption for us. For if the blood of bulls and of goats, and the ashes of an heifer sprinkling the unclean, sanctifieth to the purifying of the flesh: How much more shall the blood of Christ, who through the eternal Spirit offered himself without spot to God, purge your conscience from dead works to serve the living God?"*

The Christian does not need a confessor to purge his conscience, or a mediator between him and God. We read in 1 Timothy 2:5-6, *"For there is one God, and one mediator between God and men, the man Christ Jesus; Who gave himself a ransom for all, to be testified in due time."*

The Roman emperors continued to hold the spiritual office of the Supreme Pontiff until Gratian refused it in 376 A.D. He believed the position to be idolatrous and un-Christian. So, in 378 A.D. Demasus, bishop of Rome, was given the title of Pontifex Maximus. Thereafter, within Christendom the office of a high priest, with a lower caste of supporting priesthood, was established. This system has been carried on in various branches of Christianity to this day. But such a religious system has no scriptural foundation. It is more Babylonish in origin and tradition than Christian. In fact, the garments of the high priest and the order of priesthood are very similar to those of the religion of Babylon.

Supposedly, the basis for the office of a high priest within Christendom is the tradition that Simon Peter established when he went to Rome. However, there is absolutely no scriptural evidence that Peter was ever in Rome. Peter was sent as an apostle to the Jews, while Paul was sent to the Gentiles. Considerable evidence has been presented that the Simon who was in Rome was actually Simon the sorcerer of Acts 8. The *Catholic Encyclopedia* states of this Simon:

> *"Justin Martyr and other early writers inform us that he afterward went to Rome, worked miracles there by the power of demons, and received divine honors both in Rome and in his own country. Though much extravagant legend afterward gathered around the name of this Simon . . . it seems nevertheless probable that there must be some foundation in fact for the account given by Justin and accepted by Eusebius. The historical Simon Magus no doubt founded some sort of religion as a*

*counterfeit of Christianity in which he claimed
to play a part analogous to that of Christ."*

After the office of Pontifex Maximus was vacated by Gratian, it became strictly a religious position within Christendom. Nevertheless, under the doctrine of Divine Right of Kings, no ruler or king of Europe could be crowned without the blessing and coronation by this supreme religious authority. The intrigue and power struggle between the crowned heads of Europe and the central religious authority in Rome are well recorded in European history.

In the year 800 A.D., Pope Leo III crowned Charlemagne emperor of Rome and gave him the holy mission of unifying all Christendom under the authority of the church. With the decline and fall of the Roman Empire, over the next four centuries this authority was transferred to Germany. According to Edward Crankshaw, author of *The Fall Of the House of Hapsburg*, this divine duty was conferred upon Rudolf, Count of Hapsburg, the emperor of the Germans, in 1283 A.D. Again, the wars and efforts of the Hapsburgs to weld a Holy Roman Empire of Europe are history.

A contemporary successor to Count Rudolf Hapsburg is Otto Von Hapsburg, a member of the Common Market Parliament, who made the following observation in 1984:

*"If Iran collapses in its war with Iraq,
there will be a chain reaction all through the*

Middle East. . . . The Shiites believe that the twelfth Imman (successor to Mohammed) is coming back. They believe that this Mahdi — their messiah — is about to approach, that there will be a united world directed by the Shiites, that Khomeini is the prophet of the approaching Mahdi. . . . Europe too has a right to be decolonized. That is our responsibility toward those of Eastern Europe. . . . It is our duty to see to it that one day they shall have an opportunity to exercise their right of self-determination (in the European Parliament). . . . This is the reason we must strive for a political Europe. . . . Back in the events of politics is still a moral and mental attitude. The religious foundation of a society is the only real and lasting foundation that this society may have . . . to return truly and fully again to the roots of our greatness. . . . We are already in a political Europe. . . . We are well beyond the point of no return. . . . We have not yet arrived at the other shore; but we can't go back.

The return of Europe to the religious roots of its greatness could only refer to the concept of the unification of a political Europe, the revived Roman Empire under a single religious authority. The first major breakdown in papal authority over the kings of Europe came in 1527 when King Henry VIII of England was successful in terminating the authority of Rome over the British throne. The aftermath of the Protestant Reformation further weakened the ties between the royal families of Europe and Rome. However, though somewhat dormant, the ambition to exercise religious dictation to the kings of the earth has remained a cherished goal. Today, each of over one hundred nations, including the United States, has an ambassador to the Vatican. We have presented this information as a possible explanation of the religious system called Mystery Babylon in Revelation. But as we also read in Revelation, after the system has worked to bring all the false religions of the world to worship the Antichrist as god, it will be destroyed. *"And the ten horns which thou sawest upon the beast, these shall hate the whore, and shall make her desolate and naked, and shall eat her flesh, and burn her with fire. For God hath put in their hearts to fulfil his will, and to agree, and give their kingdom unto the beast, until the words of God shall be fulfilled. And the woman which thou sawest is that great city, which reigneth over the kings of the earth"* (Rev. 17:16-18).

We are in no way stating that the Babylonish system of religion is centered in one specific church or faith. However, it is consolidated in some more than others. At the beginning of Babel the religious system was to serve Nimrod the king. In the city of Babylon the same was true. In Daniel 2 we find that Nebuchadnezzar demanded that the Chaldean priesthood and the leaders of the occult reveal to him a dream that he had dreamed.

When they failed, he decreed that they all be killed. In Babylon, the king was head of everything, including the birds of the air and the beasts of the field.

The image the king saw in his dream represented the "times of the Gentiles." This period extended from the reign of Nebuchadnezzar to the coming of the Messiah to set up an everlasting kingdom. Babylon was the first Gentile kingdom. Daniel pointed to Nebuchadnezzar and said, "Thou art this head of gold." The head controls the rest of the body, and the Babylonish system will determine the course of Gentile empires until a king, like Nebuchadnezzar, will gain power over all nations, peoples, commerce, wealth, and everything that lives. We read in Revelation 13:7-9: *"And it was given unto him to make war with the saints, and to overcome them: and power was given him over all kindreds, and tongues, and nations. And all that dwell upon the earth shall worship him, whose names are not written in the book of life of the Lamb slain from the foundation of the world. If any man have an ear, let him hear."*

It would appear the religious system of the last Babylon is also in view in Revelation 18:7-8, *"How much she hath glorified herself, and lived deliciously, so much torment and sorrow give her: for she saith in her heart, I sit a queen, and am no widow, and shall see no sorrow. Therefore shall her plagues come in one day, death, and mourning, and famine; and she shall be utterly burned with fire: for strong is the Lord God who judgeth her."*

It is our understanding of Scripture that the true church, the Bride of Christ, will be taken out of the world at the beginning of the tribulation period. Mystery Babylon, the mother of harlots, will be left waiting at the altar. But she attaches herself to another love, the Antichrist, and boasts that she is no widow — she reigns as a queen of the beast empire. She assumes the position of Semiramis, the queen of heaven. As the saints of the tribulation are killed for not worshipping the Antichrist and receiving his mark, she thinks that no such sorrow will come to her. But suddenly, even as Nebuchadnezzar almost destroyed the religious system of Babylon in his day, a decree comes from the Antichrist for the kings of his empire to destroy every vestige of the religious element.

In his book *Hidden Prophecies In the Psalms*, Rev. J.R. Church developed a pattern of prophecies that have been fulfilled in the twentieth century. Beginning with Psalm 1 he shows how a prophecy in that psalm was fulfilled in the year 1901. He then continues psalm by psalm, and we notice that Babylon is mentioned in Psalm 87:1-4: *"His foundation is in the holy mountains. The Lord loveth the gates of Zion more than all the dwellings of Jacob. Glorious things are spoken of thee, O city of God. Selah. I will make mention of Rahab and Babylon to them that know me: behold Philistia, and Tyre, with Ethiopia; this man was born there."*

God loves Jerusalem, the city of Zion, more than all the cities of the world where Jacob is still scattered today. And as the psalm indicates, the major concern of Israel today is the growing population of the Arab-Palestinians who are clamoring for independent status.

Tyre, which is in Lebanon, is still a major problem to the state of Israel. Ethiopia to the south of Israel refers to the threat of the invasion of Russia with an alliance of nations that surround Israel — Libya, Iran, and Ethiopia. The psalmist also wrote: *"I will make mention of Rahab and Babylon to them that know me."*

Rev. Church says of this passage in Psalm 87:

> *"The psalmist referred to Rahab, a notorious harlot in the days of Joshua, connecting her with the mystery religion of ancient Babylon. It seems that God has thus promised to reveal the harlot Babylon to those who desire to know the mystery. The Apostle John called her MYSTERY, BABYLON THE GREAT, THE MOTHER OF HARLOTS AND ABOMINATIONS OF THE EARTH (Rev. 17:5). To this day, BABYLON THE GREAT has remained a mystery. Perhaps soon, however, she will be revealed."*

When Rev. Church wrote his commentary on Psalm 87, the month-long festival in Babylon — to let the world know that the city lives again — had not been announced. This event, of course, adds new meaning to this psalm. It is also interesting that we read in Psalm 89:10: *"Thou hast broken Rahab in pieces, as one that is slain. . . ."* The breaking of Rahab in pieces could refer to the judgment mentioned in Revelation that is determined for Babylon in the last days.

Chapter Seven

U.S.A. and Babylon

Dr. S. Franklin Logsdon in his book *Is the U.S.A. In Prophecy?* states:

"*The Babylon matter is comprehended within three designations:*

Historical Babylon in Genesis 11
Ecclesiastical Babylon in Revelation 7
Political Bablyon in Revelation 18

Historical Babylon will ultimately manifest itself in two imposing branches — the false church and a powerful God-forsaken nation. . . . Historical Babylon is symbolized by a monumental tower, Ecclesiastical Babylon by a mythical woman, and Political Babylon by a mighty city. The aim is, respectively, to reach heaven, to rob heaven, and to reject heaven. The proposal of the first was a common language. The proposal of the second is a common worship. The proposal of the third is a common privilege — one speech, one church, one society. . . . In the case of Historical Babylon, God felled the tower, confounded the tongues, and scattered the people. In the case of Ecclesiastical or Religious Babylon, the Antichrist will hate the harlot (the false church), outlaw religion, and finally kill the "woman"; that is, he will destroy the final development of organized religion. In the case of prophesied Political Babylon, trials will plague the earth, the economy will crash, the great city will be made desolate.

Babylonism is not only a system of contradictory works, but a scheme of unmitigated robbery, depriving the infinite God of the praise and glory due His holy name, denying His power and His operations. . . . God, who established His battalions in the skies, from before the foundation of the world, has set the exact time for each of His inevitable victories over these forces of unrighteousness. He will eliminate utterly the false church through the agency of Antichrist or the coming world dictator (Rev. 17:17). He will also completely destroy a powerful end-time nation which is spiritually called Babylon (Rev. 18:10). The word end-time connotes the closing days of the present order of things.

Many other prophetic observers, like Dr. Logsdon, see in the destruction of Babylon at the end of the age a mystery religion, a mystery economic system, a mystery city, and a mystery nation. And, Dr. Logsdon and others have reached the conclusion that the mystery nation is the United States. As objectionable and unpatriotic as this presumption may appear to us, this viewpoint is worthy of careful consideration.

That God loves America is not the point in question here. Our nation was founded on a strong biblical foundation. Our first settlers came here to find a land where they could worship God in spirit and in truth. God is recognized in our supreme law of the land, our Constitution; we have given a home to the homeless; churches dot the landscape in every city; we have sent Christian missionaries to all nations; and the United States has been a refuge for God's earthly people, the Jews. We fully believe that God does love America, but God also loved Israel. The biblical precept is: To whom much is given, much is required.

During the coming Great Tribulation, the Antichrist will be the ruler of all nations, none excepted. We read in Micah 5:15, *"I will execute vengeance in anger and fury upon the heathen. . . ."* We read also in Ezekiel 39:21, *". . . and all the heathen shall see my judgment. . . ."* Likewise Obadiah 15: *"For the day of the Lord is near upon all the heathen. . . ."* And Revelation 19:15: *"And out of his mouth goeth a sharp sword, that with it he should smite the nations. . . ."* Without doubt, the United States will be a partaker in the destructive judgments that will come upon all nations in the last days.

Going back to the foundations of Babylon, the primary reason for the building of the Tower of Babel was to build a tower with a top to reach into Heaven. The two nations that have opened a gateway to the heavens through a space program are Russia and the United States, but it is significant that the United States has been the only nation to send human beings to another heavenly body — the moon.

According to the prophetic description of the nation of Babylon in the end-time, that nation will be identified by a great city. According to the 1986 *World Almanac*, New York City, consisting of five boroughs, is still the largest city in the world with a population of 15,791,214. New York City is allegorically called "the Babylon on the Hudson." On Long Island, across from mainland New York City, is Babylon, New York, zip code 11702, with a population of 12,897 in 1980. At the entrance to New York City is our most emblemic national monument, the Statue of Liberty. Irregardless of the spiritual significance we, and the rest of the world, may subscribe to the Statue of Liberty, it is interesting to note that it is approximately the same height as the idol Nebuchadnezzar erected on the plains of Dura. Nebuchadnezzar's image was sixty cubits high, or one hundred ten feet, by using the most common measurement of 1.824 feet for a cubit. The Statue of Liberty is one hundred eleven feet high. In 1986 a rededication of the Statue of Liberty took place; the rededication of Babylon occured in 1987. Just as the image of Nebuchadnezzar in Babylon was one foot shorter than the Statue of Liberty, the rededication of the Statue of Liberty, accompanied by one of the most elaborate celebrations the United States has ever witnessed, fell one year short of the massive celebration for the revival of Babylon.

We have previously commented in some detail concerning the identification of the obelisk with the worship of Nimrod and the mystery Babylon religious system. According to Ralph Woodrow, as stated in *Babylon Mystery Religion*, two of the highest obelisk structures in the world are the tower of the great Cathedral of Cologne, which is five hundred twelve feet high, and the tower of the Cathedral of Ulm, which is five hundred twenty-eight feet high — both in Germany. However, the tallest obelisk in all the world is on a small hill in front of our nation's capitol building, the Washington Monument, which is five hundred fifty-five and a half feet tall. This national monument was built in honor of the father of our country, George Washington. The Washington Monument is open to the public three hundred sixty-four days a year; the only day it is closed is Christmas Day, the day when Christians remember the birth of Jesus Christ.

Many of the prophecies in the Bible have double meanings. We notice this fact especially in Isaiah where most prophecies about the coming Messiah refer to His first coming as Savior to offer Himself as an offering for sin, and then again to His second coming to establish His kingdom on earth. Jeremiah 50 and 51 relate to God's judgment of Babylon. Some of the verses in these chapters refer to the Babylon of Jeremiah's day, while others refer to the final destruction of Babylon. They could not all refer to the Babylon of the sixth century B.C., because the sudden and ultimate destruction as foretold by Jeremiah is in the day of the Lord's vengeance upon the earth, and in the day when Israel will return from all nations seeking the Lord their God.

We read in Jeremiah 50:37, *"A sword is upon . . . the mingled people that are in the midst of her. . . ."* It was at Babel that God confounded the language of mankind and scattered the people over the face of the earth. At Babylon, Nebuchadnezzar sought to reverse God's decree for the division of races and nations. In each race, there are distinctive skills and abilities inherent to a particular nation or race. At Babylon the young scientists from Judah were among those brought to the country, and those having particular skills, talents, and aptitudes from all nations were congregated once more to incorporate collective knowledge in building a kingdom that Nebuchadnezzar thought would endure forever. Quoting from *Everyday Life In Babylonia and Assyria:*

> *"The population of Babylon was a very mixed one, both racially and socially. As to race, Nebuchadnezzar impressed labour gangs for his public works in Babylon from the whole of his empire. Many of these were no doubt only too glad to return to their native lands . . . but others certainly stayed for good in Babylon, either settling down with wives who had followed them from their homeland or marrying*

local women. Such foreign settlers were no more than the most recent importation of foreign blood. There were many other peoples who during the preceding centuries had been in the city, whether as conquerors, captives, or just visitors, long enough to interbreed with Babylonian ladies. Amongst these were Cassites, Hittites, Elamites, and an occasional Egyptian, Arameans, Assyrians, Chaldeans, and, in the reign of Nebuchadnezzar himself, Jews. Babylon was a thoroughly mongrel city."

The United States, like Babylon, is a mongrel nation. The first settlers in America were English. By 1790 almost two hundred years later, ninety percent of the population was still English and Scotch, with ten percent being from Germany, Holland, Ireland, and France. The rising slave trade was responsible for bringing hundreds of thousands of the Negro race from Africa; famine in Ireland brought many more from Ireland; the need for cheap labor to build the railroads brought the Chinese. Political and religious persecutions in Russia resulted in thousands more coming from the Ukraine. Jews came to escape persecution and for better business opportunities. The aftermath of World War II saw many more come. By 1980 more than one million Cubans had migrated to escape communism; the Vietnam War caused an influx of millions of Vietnamese, Cambodians, and Laotians. And so they have come from all over the world — from India, Japan, Sweden, Poland, and all nations. And, like Babylon, after World War II we brought in German scientists to help build our space program. Currently, the biggest influx is from Central America to escape from war in that area, and thousands cross our border from Mexico. Quoting *The Immigration Time Bomb* by Palmer Stacy and Wayne Lutton:

> *"America is being invaded. Every day thousands of foreigners illegally enter our country. Over two million illegal aliens will come this year, most of them penetrating our porous two thousand-mile border with Mexico. Additional hundreds of thousands will arrive through our superficially inspected harbors and international airports. In 1975, General Leonard Chapman, Commissioner of the Immigration and Naturalization Service, warned: 'Illegal immigration is out of control.' The total number of illegal aliens already in the United States may exceed twelve million — more than twice the size of the Soviet armed forces. President Ronald Reagan stated on October 19, 1983, that 'this country has lost control of its own borders, and no country can sustain that kind of position.'"*

There are now so many languages spoken in our country it is almost like Babel after the confusion of tongues. Some states are considering laws to maintain education and communications in our common English language. Babylon used people from other nations to help build a mighty nation, but in the end the foreigners proved a detriment to survival. This is not to say Americans should not be proud of their heritage in being a refuge of safety for the oppressed and downtrodden, but on the other hand, we have indeed become much like ancient Babylon.

Edward Tracy, in his book *The United States In Prophecy*, wrote:

> *It was the solemn judgment of God that of one language and one people there should be many languages and many peoples. The motto of the United States is 'E Pluribus Unum,' which means 'Out of many, one.' Intentional or not, this is nothing less than effrontery, if you recall that lest the people of Babel should exalt themselves against God, He said, in effect, 'Out of one, many.' . . .*
>
> *"Having a political structure which is tantamount to a reversal of God's singular judgment against Babel, this country has certainly not been restrained from doing all that which they have been able to imagine — even so far as going to the moon."*

Keeping in mind that Jeremiah 50 and 51 has a double application to old Babylon and the last Babylon, we read Jeremiah 50:12, *"Your mother shall be sore confounded; she that bare you shall be ashamed; behold, the hindermost of the nations shall be a wilderness, a dry land, and a desert."* The mother of the United States is England, and our nation did indeed confound England in the War of Independence. The reference to the "hindermost of the nations" does not mean the least of the nations, but rather the last of the nations, or a new nation. In Jeremiah's time this could mean Babylon, except the land of the nation of Babylon has never become a wilderness and a desert. The land between the Tigris and Euphrates rivers is still one of the richest agricultural regions in the world; only the city declined and became mostly uninhabited over a time period of about six hundred years. In an end-time setting, the hindermost or newest of the great nations would, of course, be the United States.

Another verse in Jeremiah 50 gives another clue that Babylon could possibly be the United States: *"How is the hammer of the whole earth cut asunder and broken! how is Babylon become a desolation among the nations!"* (Jer. 50:23). A hammer is a carpenter's tool to drive nails. To hammer a person means to beat them down so they will submit to your will. In the way it is used in Jeremiah 50:23, it means to fashion or shape; in reference to a nation, its usage infers a powerful political force in the world. Since World War II, the United States has been the hammer among nations, at least the free world. At Potsdam, Franklin D. Roosevelt met with Joseph Stalin to hammer out the shape of the post-war world. Eastern Europe was given to Russia, and the colonial empires of Europe, including England, were broken up. Winston Churchill was quoted as saying that he refused to be a partner in any political agreement that would bring about the dissolution of the British Empire. Nevertheless, the United States prevailed. After the war, the United States reshaped Europe through NATO, the Common Market, and the Marshall Foreign Aid Plan, which made West Germany a major industrial power. In the Orient, the United States helped to make Japan the most industrialized nation the world has ever seen. In Southeast Asia our hammer was dented, but we still have enough political prestige to affect the political shape of the Middle East. This is not to criticize our efforts to contain communism and help to shape a better world, but most of our foreign diplomatic attempts either backfire or come to nought. As it was at Babylon, so it still is today — it is God who rules in the affairs of men and nations and even sets over them the basest of men.

There are many parallels between the religious, commercial, and national Babylon of the last days and the United States. Only the unfolding of future events can verify this comparison. However, with the rise of Iraq to a military power of dimensions to cause a mobilization of many nations and threaten world peace, the emphasis of prophetic interpretation shifts back to the site of the once mighty world empire ruled by Nebuchadnezzar.

Chapter Eight

Iraq — Prelude To Armageddon

On March 29, 1971, an AP news release from Beirut, Lebanon reported:

> *"Babylon Plan Set — Iraq says it plans to rebuild the ancient city of Babylon, whose hanging gardens were among the seven wonders of the world. The project will cost about $30 million."*

We determined to travel to Iraq and see for ourselves this ancient city of Nebuchadnezzar that was rising from the dust of history. So, on March 13, 1978, after a breakfast of Iraqi bread and fig preserves, served with thick, black, bitter coffee, the ninety-seven members of a tour group that I was leading boarded buses and headed out of Baghdad for Babylon on the Euphrates. We traveled westward at sixty-five miles an hour over a four-lane highway, passing kilns along the way that were turning out bricks for the reconstruction project.

Archaeologists had already excavated much of the ruins. The Germans had even removed the upper portion of the Ishtar Gate and reassembled it in a museum in Berlin. But large sections of the city were still recognizable, and it appeared that from five to ten percent of the buildings were in the process of being restored. While in Iraq we went south to see the city of Ur, the home of Abraham. We also went north to Nineveh and saw the remains of this once mighty metropolis.

Just before our arrival in Iraq, Israel launched a military campaign into Lebanon to clean out PLO terrorist groups, so the entire Middle East was on war footing. We were supposed to have taken sleeper cars to Nineveh, but the Iraqi government was using these facilities to move troops by train through Turkey and Syria into Lebanon. So our group was given two coach cars, hooked on to an ammunition and troop train. We were told to stay put in our seats and not move. I still remember the Iraqi military police walking up and down the aisles, all night long, beating their palms with huge baseball bat-like clubs. We needed little additional incentive to keep us very still and quiet.

Saddam Hussein's (Black) Golden Image

Nebuchanezzar was informed by Daniel that he was the head of gold on the image the king saw in his dream (Dan. 2). But, the head of gold was to give way to three succeeding kingdoms. This displeased the king, so he subsequently made an entire image of gold. This was Nebuchadnezzar's way of showing Daniel's God that his kingdom would last forever; and his city, Babylon, would be an eternal city.

History confirms that in 538 B.C. Daniel's prophecy regarding the fall of Babylon to the Medo-Persian Empire came to pass. But the monetary factor that figures in the rebuilding of Babylon today is not yellow gold, but black gold — oil. Oil, according to the explanation given by many geologists, is the decayed residue of plant and animal life. The one place in all the world that has more oil than any other is the small country of Kuwait, the site of the biblical Garden of Eden. This means that where Kuwait is today, there must at one time have been a veritable jungle. From this vast oil pool center, lesser pools spread out into southern Iraq, southern Iran, and northeast Saudi Arabia. Within an area roughly encompassing a circle two hundred miles in diameter, with the center in Kuwait, lies over fifty percent of the world's oil reserves.

When we traveled through Iraq in 1978 army camps were much in evidence. Soldiers were everywhere, and from the highways we could see armored columns training for combat. Most of the armaments at that time came from Russia. Iraq is an area roughly the size of California, with a population of 17 million — 75 percent Arab; 15 percent Kurd; 10 percent Turk and others. The size of the nation's present army is given at one million. During the Nixon and Ford administrations the U.S. State Department became concerned about Iraq's growing militarism and close alliance with Russia. Agents from the CIA convinced the Kurds, who had a natural hostility toward the Arabs anyway, to begin guerilla activities in the north with pledged U.S. support. But then, Henry Kissinger negotiated a favorable oil deal with Baghdad. No support came from the U.S. and the poor Kurds were offered like sacrificial lambs — rebel leaders were hanged and thousands of others were shot. These are the same Kurds that Saddam Hussein killed with nerve gas and mustard gas during the war with Iran. Much of the problem this nation is now facing in the Middle East is of our own making.

In 1978 as we traveled to southern Iraq, the closer we came to Ur, the more evident oil fields became. But what did the main items of interest that we saw in Iraq (oil fields, rebuilding of Babylon, and advancing militarism) have in common?

The perpetuation of a Babylonian (Babel) kingdom with an eternal city as the pearl of Chaldean pride has never died in the minds and hearts of the descendants of the royal family of ancient Babylon. The seating of Saddam Hussein as the sole dictator of Iraq in 1979 revived the image of Nebuchadnezzar. In fact, Saddam Hussein claims to be a reincarnation of Nebuchadnezzar, and on the bricks used to rebuild Babylon the names of both (Nebuchadnezzar and Saddam Hussein) appear side by side in the baked clay.

It may be debated as to whether the motivation for the building of a relatively small nation into a military superpower was for aggression or the pursuit of the dream of Nebuchadnezzar to control the world, and to be worshipped by all nations as a god. But if the gaining of territory and power was the only objective, why spend hundreds of millions of dollars (the first $30 million was only a drop in the bucket) to rebuild an ancient city with evidently no commercial or military importance.

The most valuable commodity in the world to mankind, is of course, fresh water. The second most important is food. The third most valuable item to the contemporary social and economic structure is energy — energy to provide heating, cooling, lighting, machine power, automobile and airplane transportation. Oil is the best source of energy. Of the industrial powers, Japan and Europe import practically one hundred percent of their oil, and the United States imports over fifty percent of the oil needed. If the world would pay $30 a barrel for oil as it did in the oil crisis of the 1970s, then it would just as readily pay $100 a barrel if forced to do so. Saddam Hussein reasoned that the man who could control the world's oil market could become the most powerful man on earth, and over fifty percent of the world's oil was at his doorstep.

Presidents Johnson, Nixon, and Ford had built the army of the Shah of Iran into the third most powerful military force in the world. But President Carter had practically abolished the CIA and the revolution that overthrew the Shah caught him by surprise. He was too indecisive to react. Then followed the humiliating capture and imprisonment of Americans as hostages. The United States was hailed as the Great Satan by Khomeini and the Ayatollah became the most despised man by the free world.

Saddam Hussein of Iraq then seized this opportunity

to add the oil fields of Iran to his kingdom on the road to glory. Although Saddam Hussein reasoned that Iran would be an easy pushover, he did not reckon with an army that had been trained and equipped by the United States. For eight long years, as long as World War I and World War II combined, Iran and Iraq fought to a standstill. The main difference between the two antagonists was that Iraq had more outside support. Saddam Hussein had unlimited credit to buy weapons on the world market, and the battlefield became a training ground for his army. President Reagan and the U.S. State Department even explained away as an accident a missile attack by Iraq on a Navy vessel in which American lives were lost. Also overlooked, conveniently, was the unmerciful killing of innocent civilians, including the Kurds in Iraq, with poison gas. Saddam Hussein literally got away with murder. Although the war with Iran ended in a stalemate, Saddam emerged as the winner in the eyes of the world. While he did not get much oil, he did salvage a few pieces of Iran's territory.

One nation that was never deceived by Saddam Hussein's long-range plans for rebuilding the Babylonian Empire was Israel. In 1981 Israel made an air strike against a nuclear plant in Iraq to prevent the development of atomic and hydrogen bombs. Had Israel not destroyed this nuclear facility, Iraq might today have nuclear weapons, which would make the present situation far more dangerous. That the Iraqi dictator is still trying to make nuclear weapons is quite clear from the attempt to funnel atomic bomb parts to Baghdad through

England. Shortly afterward another attempt was made by Saddam Hussein to import parts for a huge howitzer that would propel a projectile capable of delivering nerve gas or an atomic warhead distances of up to five thousand miles. The man responsible was an ordinance expert whose plans for such an enormous gun had been rejected by the U.S. Army. He evidently sold the idea to Hussein, but then the inventor himself was assassinated in Brussels in March. When in Israel in June 1990, I inquired as to whether Mossad operators or CIA agents had terminated the man, but I was told the killing was probably done by Iraqi agents when the deal began to go sour.

Although Saddam Hussein has not been able to obtain super terror weapons, other than poison gas, he evidently felt there was no one who would dare challenge his move to take over Kuwait. Only an unprecedented quick response by President George Bush kept the Iraq army from continuing on south and capturing the Saudi oil fields. Saddam Hussein now controls thirty-two percent of the world's oil reserves; had he gotten the oil fields of Saudi Arabia, he would have controlled over fifty percent, and possibly become the most powerful man on earth. He could have created havoc in the industrialized world.

Other Interested Participants

The United Nations Security Council, realizing the danger presented by Saddam Hussein to the most valuable energy source on earth, quickly voted embargo sanctions against Iraq. The Arab League failed to offer any acceptable solution, but some have offered help or sent token forces to join the Americans in Saudi Arabia:

Iran: Iran has a population of 51 million with a standing army of 604,000. However, Iran's military hardware has been wasted in the eight-year war with Iraq. Presently, Iran has only five hundred old tanks and one hundred twenty airplanes of questionable service. Iran's ability to wage other than defensive warfare is highly suspect. While President Rafsanjani has given tacit support of the U.S-U.N. campaign to stop Saddam Hussein, recent overtures to Iran by Iraq to release all Iranian prisoners and return back all territory taken in the recent war indicates that a deal has been made. If Iran makes up with its former enemy, or even assumes a benign neutrality, then the embargo against Iraq will be difficult to enforce and Hussein can divert 300,000 soldiers protecting his eastern front elsewhere.

Syria: Syria has a population of 12 million with a standing army of 404,000. Although Iraq's army is much larger numerically, the Syrian army can match the Iraqis in armaments with four thousand tanks and five hundred airplanes. The Syrian divisions are mobile and well-trained by the Russians. Assad and Saddam Hussein are old enemies and Syria has committed a troop contingent to defend Saudi Arabia alongside the Americans. However, as far as Assad and Saddam Hussein are concerned, there is little to choose between them. A few years ago my tour group stopped in Homs, located in the north of Syria, for lunch. The people were friendly and we were mobbed by students wanting to meet Americans and try out their English. A few months later, Assad sent his extermination squads into Homs and murdered fifteen thousand innocent civilians. Both Assad and Saddam Hussein are known for pulling their pistols and blowing the brains out of anyone who questions their authority as object lessons to others. However, recently Assad has attempted to mend his image and appear as a more moderate leader.

Jordan: Although Jordan is five times the size of Israel in area, the country has a population of only 3 million. The Jordanian army has less than 100,000 soldiers, equipped with approximately one thousand tanks and one hundred airplanes. Jordan has profited from both the chaos in Lebanon and war between Iran and Iraq. Middle East banking establishments moved from Beirut to Amman, and Saddam Hussein spent billions in Jordan to build the four-lane Desert Road, a five hundred-mile super-highway running the length of the country down to the port of Aqaba. King Hussein has built Amman into a modern, beautiful city, but suddenly the outside funds dried up. When we were in Jordan in June 1990, the dinar had lost almost thirty percent of its value in just the previous six months. King Hussein's neck is on the block because his seat is on an uneasy throne. The king stated while we were in Amman that he would welcome unification with Iraq, and this is why he has offered excuses for Saddam Hussein in the invasion of Kuwait. Israel has served notice in the event of such a unification, immediate war would result, because the Jews could not tolerate the Iraqi army camped on the east bank of the Jordan.

Others: Turkey is a member of NATO with a well-trained and equipped army. In battle, the Turks have always proven to be fearless warriors. Turkey has initially pledged to support the embargo against Iraq. The same can be said of Egypt, which is sending support troops to Saudi Arabia, and ditto for Morocco. Libya is an unknown quantity, but Quadafy is the godfather of international terrorism and could create problems down the road. Sabri al-Banna, better known as Abu Nidal, has reportedly joined other terrorist leaders in Baghdad. However, a report in the August 11, 1990 edition of the *Jerusalem Post* presents evidence that Abu Nidal has been terminated by Quadafy. Why? Because Abu had become mentally unstable, killing all twenty of his senior lieutenants at a secret meeting in Tripoli, and then later ordering the klling of one hundred of his support terrorist groups in Lebanon. This also illustrates the cruelty and unpredictability of the Arab mentality, and this applies not only to Nidal, Quadafy, Assad, and Saddam Hussein, but to all Arab national leaders. Mubarak of Egypt recently stated for U.S. national television news thusly:

> *"Arab loyalties and alliances are like the wind. You may expect that tomorrow they will change."*

Israel: Israel has a well-trained and well-equipped

army of almost 700,000 men and women, backed by four thousand tanks and six hundred airplanes. Israel is the only stable U.S. ally in the Middle East. Saddam Hussein hopes to pull Israel into the current crisis in order to turn all other Arab nations against the United States. A Reuter news release reported on August 12, 1990: "A statement issued by the group [The World Islamic League] after an appeal by Saddam Hussein to Arabs and Moslems to save the Holy Places of Mecca and Medina from foreign forces said, 'We wish Iraqi President Saddam Hussein would call on Arabs and Moslems to liberate al-Aqsa Mosque from Jewish hands.' " Of course, al-Aqsa Mosque stands on the Temple Mount in Jerusalem, and this illustrates how unstable and dangerous the position of U.S. troops are in Saudi Arabia.

Other Fair-Weather Friends and Questionable Allies: Japan and the Common Market nations have more at stake in the Middle East than any other nation or group of nations. Yet, as usual, they seem to be standing around looking up at the sky while the United States pulls their chestnuts out of the fire, and the American taxpayers foot the bill. However, Russian intentions in the Middle East are still highly suspect.

What Does the Bible Say?

Bible prophecy in some respects is like watching a ninety-minute movie which covers a fifty-year timespan. A time segment of ten, twenty, or thirty years may be omitted from the movie because what happened during that time is not essential to the main story. For example, in Isaiah 61 the prophet sees Christ at His first coming to die for sin and then goes immediately to His second coming as the King of Glory.

In many prophecies relating to Babylon, the nation is described in its glory under Nebuchadnezzar, its fall to the Medes and Persians, and then its ultimate destruction: *"The noise of a multitude in the mountains, like as of a great people; a tumultuous noise of the kingdoms of nations gathered together: the Lord of hosts mustereth the host of the battle. They come from a far country, from the end of heaven, even the Lord, and the weapons of his indignation, to destroy the whole land. Howl ye; for the day of the Lord is at hand; it shall come as a destruction from the Almighty . . . And Babylon, the glory of kingdoms, the beauty of the Chaldees' excellency, shall be as when God overthrew Sodom and Gomorrah. It shall never be inhabited . . ."* (Isa. 13:4-6, 19-20).

When Babylon fell to the Medes and Persians in 538 B.C. the city itself was taken without a fight. The physical structure of Babylon was not changed. It remained an important metropolis during the Medo-Persian Empire, and it was Alexander the Great's headquarters. It was here that Alexander died in 320 B.C. Many Jews remained in Babylon, and Peter wrote his first epistle from Babylon in 63 A.D. But sometime after 100 A.D. the Euphrates River changed its course and Babylon was buried under almost one hundred feet of sand. There it has remained for almost two millennia until its rebuilding by Saddam Hussein. It has never been destroyed as Sodom and Gomorrah was, and God says it will not be destroyed completely and finally until the day of the Lord. The day of the Lord always refers to the Great Tribulation and second coming of Jesus Christ. In Isaiah 13 we do read about the taking of old Babylon by the Medes and Persians, but of the final judgment in a fiery holocaust the prophet said there would first be gathered against it an army from many nations, even from the ends of the earth. Prophetically, what is happening in the Middle East today, the gathering of armies representing the U.N., an organization of one hundred sixty nations, could indicate that we're nearing the time of the coming of the Lord and the battle of Armageddon.

Next, let us consider the story of Babylon as told by Jeremiah: *"And I will bring Israel again to his habitation, and he shall feed on Carmel and Bashan* [Golan Heights], *and his soul shall be satisfied upon mount Ephraim and Gilead. In those days, and in that time, saith the Lord, the iniquity of Israel shall be sought for . . . and the sins of Judah, and they shall not be found: for I will pardon them whom I reserve . . . A sound of battle is in the land, and of great destruction. How is the hammer of the whole earth cut asunder and broken! how is Babylon become a desolation among the nations! . . . A sword is upon their horses, and upon their chariots, and upon all the mingled people that are in the midst of her . . . a sword is upon her treasures; and they shall be robbed . . . As God overthrew Sodom and Gomorrah and the neighbour cities thereof, saith the Lord; so shall no man abide there, neither shall any son of man dwell therein. Behold, a people shall come from the north, and a great nation, and many kings shall be raised up from the coasts of the earth"* (Jer. 50:19-20, 22-23, 37, 40-41).

Israel has been regathered back in the land, a remnant from among the nations, and they are dwelling even upon the old land of Bashan as prophesied. It is in these days, Jeremiah said, that God will redeem them from their sins. This has not happened as yet, because redemption will come only when they believe on the Lord Jesus Christ at His coming. But we read that in that day there will be many mingled people in Babylon who will be robbed and suffer the judgment that will come upon Babylon unless they are able to flee out of the land. Today in Iraq and Kuwait there are millions living there from other nations — 2 million Egyptians alone. Some have been able to flee to safety, but most remain and will doubtless become hostages. Reports indicate that some foreign nationals are already being raped and robbed. The Iraqi army is reported to have taken up to $10 billion in gold alone from the banks in Kuwait. The future does not look good for the three thousand Americans left in Iraq and Kuwait, and all Christians should pray for their safety and deliverance.

We notice also that Jeremiah said that God would raise up against Babylon many nations from the coasts of the earth, including specifically a "great nation." We must ponder if this great nation is not the United States.

And, the gathering of all these nations from the ends of the earth could not possibly refer to the fall of Babylon in 538 B.C. at the hands of only two nations, Media and Persia. We also note that Jeremiah agrees with Isaiah, that Babylon will be destroyed like Sodom and Gomorrah, with a great noise and a moving of the earth. We also read in Revelation 18:9, 17 that Babylon will be destroyed in one hour and made desolate in a fiery holocaust. And the fact that no man or beast will be able to dwell there after the judgment indicates nuclear bombs. According to the consensus by world military experts as reported in an August 7, 1990 news review by Reuter news service, U.S. support against Iraq will be only of a token nature, and if the United States has any military effect against Saddam Hussein, it will have to be by non-conventional, or nuclear weaponry. We read also from the August 11, 1990 edition of the *Jerusalem Post*:

> *"Former defense minister Yitshak Rabin said . . . that nothing short of non-conventional arms could stop Iraq in the wake of its invasion of Kuwait. 'The armies of Iraq and Syria can compare with the armies of any European power or combination of powers in terms of size. . . . In fact, neither of the two superpowers is capable of overcoming the Iraqi army today, unless it deploys non-conventional weapons.'"*

Now, of the ruler of the Babylon that will suffer

sudden judgment, we read in Jeremiah 50:43-44 he will stand up against the armies of nations like the swelling of the Jordan. In other words, he will boast and brag and appear to be great, but in the end his courage will fail and he will become as weak as a woman in childbirth.

Scenario for Armageddon

I wrote in the December 1987 edition of *The Gospel Truth*:

> *"Three years ago the Association of Atomic Scientists in their monthly bulletin moved the hands on their 'Doomsday Clock' to four minutes until midnight. In the same edition of their publication, the scenario for the coming atomic war, or Armageddon, which they predict will happen, was set forth. The scientists predicted that the war between Iran and Iraq would continue and intensify until other nations in the Persian area would be involved. In the course of time, within a period of five years, attempts would be made to close the gulf and the major source for the world's oil supply would be cut off. Then, naval units from the United States, and then other nations, would become involved to keep the Persian Gulf open for shipping. In desperation, either Iraq or Iran would obtain and employ a few atomic weapons. Atomic war would then spread to*

*other nations in the Middle East; Russia and
the United States would then become involved
and a nuclear holocaust would engulf the
world. It is indeed amazing how closely events
in the Persian Gulf have followed this predicted
pattern."*

While the Association of Atomic Scientists did not
guess exactly right in every detail about how the crisis in
the Persian Gulf would develop, nevertheless it has
developed, and within one year of the time frame they
projected. The Arab participants in the present Middle
East situation are already putting a price tag on their
cooperation — some kind of settlement with Israel over
East Jerusalem, the West Bank (Samaria), the Temple
Mount, and the Golan Heights. It is already projected
that U.S. and U.N. forces in the Middle East will see a
prolonged stay, possibly years. We agree with Jordan's
King Hussein in one of his observations: "It seems the
world is headed for a single dictatorship."

It is a reasonable conclusion that only war can bring
about a definitive answer to safeguard the world's oil
supply; and that Israel must agree to a satisfactory
agreement with the Arab state in order to bring about
peace in the Middle East. Only the Bible holds the key as
to the order of these coming events.

One thing for certain is that now all the factors are
present in the Middle East to fulfill end-time tribulation
prophecy. Armies representing all nations are there;
weapons to bring about the destruction of Iraq and

Egypt (Ezek. 29) are there. *"Behold, the day of the Lord cometh . . . I will gather all nations against Jerusalem to battle; and the city shall be taken, and the houses rifled, and the women ravished . . ."* (Zech. 14:1-2). We read also in Revelation 16:16 that the armies of the kings of the earth will be gathered at Armageddon (Megiddo). According to Revelation 14:20 the battle will rage for one hundred seventy-six miles, the exact distance from Megiddo in Israel to Bozrah in Jordan, as mentioned by the prophet Isaiah.

In January 1990 the leaders of the world were hailing the millennium; now they are worrying about Armageddon. Daniel said the end would come as a flood. We are not making any rash predictions or setting any dates. It is entirely possible that a satisfactory solution will be found to the Middle East crisis, but top world leaders and military observers are not counting on it. It is most interesting how very closely the developing Middle East crisis corresponds with Bible prophecy that is to be fulfilled at the time of the coming of Jesus Christ to judge the world and bring in His kingdom from Heaven.

As we see "that day" approaching, as Christans let us heed the words of Peter to clean up our lives and be out declaring the gospel for the salvation of souls (2 Pet. 3:9-13). God is not willing that any should perish, and the only way to save lost souls from perishing is to preach the gospel so they might be saved.

"For God so loved the world, that he gave his only begotten Son, that whosoever believeth in him should

not perish, but have everlasting life" (John 3:16).

Chapter Nine
Isaiah Against Babylon

In the year 713 B.C., Hezekiah, king of Judah, suffered an extended period of illness. Goodwill ambassadors from Babylon came bearing gifts to cheer the good king during his convalescence. At that time in history Babylon was a growing city-state within the Assyrian Empire.

Hezekiah was flattered by the attention and generosity of the Babylonian visitors, and the king revealed to them the extent of his treasures. Upon arriving at the scene Isaiah, the prophet of God and advisor to the king, was extremely upset and warned Hezekiah: *"Behold, the days come, that all that is in thine house, and that which thy fathers have laid up in store unto this day, shall be carried into Babylon: nothing shall be left, saith the Lord. And of thy sons that shall issue from thee, which thou shalt beget, shall they take away; and they shall be eunuchs in the palace of the king of Babylon"* (2 Kings 20:17-18).

In the year 721 B.C. the Assyrians, with the help of Babylon, had conquered the northern kingdom of Israel. Judah was spared, but Israel was repopulated partly with Babylonians. And, one hundred years after the Babylonians came to visit Hezekiah, Isaiah's prophecy was fulfilled. In the year 607 B.C., several years after Nebuchadnezzar had overcome Judah and attempted to incorporate the nation as a province in his own empire, the Babylonian king destroyed Jerusalem and the Temple. As Isaiah also foretold, the descendants of Hezekiah, which included Daniel, were made eunuchs and served the king of Babylon. But why was Isaiah immediately disturbed and so sure of the eventual conquest of Judah by Babylon when he appeared before Hezekiah?

The obvious answer to this question would be that God had previously revealed to Isaiah the prophetic history of Babylon, even to the end of the age and the setting up of the kingdom of the Messiah on earth. This revelation concerning Babylon is recorded in Isaiah 13: *"The burden of Babylon, which Isaiah the son of Amoz did see. Lift ye up a banner upon the high mountain, exalt the voice unto them, shake the hand, that they may go into the gates of the nobles. I have commanded my sanctified ones, I have also called my mighty ones for mine anger, even them that rejoice in my highness. The noise of a multitude in the mountains, like as of a great people; a tumultuous noise of the kingdoms of nations gathered together: the Lord of hosts mustereth the host of the battle. They come from a far country, from the end of heaven, even the Lord, and the weapons of his indignation, to destroy the whole land. Howl ye; for the day of the Lord is at hand; it shall come as a destruction from the Almighty"* (Isa. 13:1-6).

Chapters thirteen through twenty-three of Isaiah

contain a message of wrath from God against nations that would attempt to prevent God's plan and purpose for Israel. Isaiah describes these series of prophecies as burdens because they lay heavy on his heart. Concerning Babylon, the prophet places the ultimate judgment in the "day of the Lord." The "day of the Lord" always means the day of the coming battle of Armageddon at the end of the age, the period of great destruction and tribulation. As the Apostle John in Revelation, Isaiah seems to be literally transported by the Spirit into the Great Tribulation. Therefore, the judgment against Babylon prophesied by Isaiah could in no way relate to the fall of Babylon to the Medes and the Persians when the inhabitants of the city were unaware for several days that the government had even changed hands.

At the coming final judgment of Babylon, the prophet sees the gathering of nations from the ends of the earth and he hears a great tumult as the armies are gathered first to destroy the "whole land." This means not just the city of Babylon, but all of Chaldea, the country we know today as Iraq. In 538 B.C. only two nations came against Babylon — the Medes (modern Afghanistan) and the Persians (modern Iran). These were immediate, bordering nations, not the multitude of nations seen by Isaiah, possibly the marshalling of forces from afar that is seen on our television sets today. I think this is what Isaiah saw, and what he attempted to describe, in the limitations of the language and military technology of his day. The subject of Isaiah 13 is total destruction; the object of destruction is the entire land of

Babylon (modern Iraq); the time period is the day of the Lord: *"Therefore shall all hands be faint, and every man's heart shall melt: And they shall be afraid: pangs and sorrows shall take hold of them; they shall be in pain as a woman that travaileth: they shall be amazed one at another; their faces shall be as flames. Behold, the day of the Lord cometh, cruel both with wrath and fierce anger, to lay the land desolate: and he shall destroy the sinners thereof out of it. For the stars of heaven and the constellations thereof shall not give their light: the sun shall be darkened in his going forth, and the moon shall not cause her light to shine. And I will punish the world for their evil, and the wicked for their iniquity; and I will cause the arrogancy of the proud to cease, and will lay low the haughtiness of the terrible"* (Isa. 13:7-11).

Let us compare the time of judgments against Babylon with the prophecy of Jesus Christ in the Olivet Discourse concerning the time for His second coming: *"And there shall be signs in the sun, and in the moon, and in the stars; and upon the earth distress of nations, with perplexity; the sea and the waves roaring; Men's hearts failing them for fear, and for looking after those things which are coming on the earth: for the powers of heaven shall be shaken. And then shall they see the Son of man coming in a cloud with power and great glory. And when these things begin to come to pass, then look up, and lift up your heads; for your redemption draweth nigh"* (Luke 21:25-28).

The prophecy of Isaiah corresponds in scope and content almost exactly with the prophecy of Jesus Christ.

Today the hearts of many are fearful of those things which may result from the growing Middle East crisis. Both Isaiah and Jesus warn of days of terrible destruction ahead, including great and fearful signs in the heavens, when these things begin to come to pass. Following the warning of terrible days of tribulation ahead, beginning with the gathering of armies against Babylon, Isaiah prophesies about personal concerns of those within the land: *"I will make a man more precious than fine gold; even a man than the golden wedge of Ophir. Therefore I will shake the heavens, and the earth shall remove out of her place, in the wrath of the Lord of hosts, and in the day of his fierce anger. And it shall be as the chased roe, and as a sheep that no man taketh up: they shall every man turn to his own people, and flee every one into his own land. Every one that is found shall be thrust through; and every one that is joined unto them shall fall by the sword. Their children also shall be dashed to pieces before their eyes; their houses shall be spoiled, and their wives ravished"* (Isa. 13:12-16).

When the Iraqi forces moved into Kuwait, one of the first things they did was to burn the money of foreigners and then rob the bank vaults of all gold. It was reported by world media sources that up to $10 billion in gold may have been sent back to Saddam Hussein in Baghdad. Saddam took a lesson from history when Nebuchadnezzar took all the gold from conquered countries and built a golden image of himself on the plains of Dura. But as indicated by Isaiah, the lives of loved ones who were trapped in Kuwait and Iraq became more precious than all the gold taken from the banks. As also reported by news sources and refugees, the houses were rifled and the women raped in the street by Iraqi soldiers.

Here in Isaiah 13 we read of the first of many warnings about foreigners trapped in Babylon when judgment falls. Isaiah warns about safety for children and women, and who can forget mothers and fathers shown on television pleading with the government of Iraq to allow the children and women to leave. While many women and children were allowed to exit the country, Saddam Hussein has threatened to use the men, and any other foreigners left behind, as human shields at military targets in the event of war. Isaiah also described those of other nations attempting to get out of Babylon to escape the coming judgment as hunted deer or uncared for sheep.

The prophet's description of the fleeing multitudes coincides exactly with the millions attempting to flee into Jordan or Turkey by any method of transportation, many hungry, lost, or dying for lack of food and water. Foreigners from many nations (Egypt, Philippines, India, United States, England, France, Germany, Austria, Turkey, Iranian prisoners of war, Pakistan, Algeria, Italy, and others who have gone to oil-rich Iraq and Kuwait to work) desperately tried to escape. Never, in the history of the world, has there been such a frantic exodus from any nation as there was in August 1990 when millions of foreigners tried to get out of Iraq by any means possible. If this was not the scene described in

Isaiah 13, then it must refer to another in the distant future, because foreign nationals are not likely to return to Iraq for years to come.

Isaiah continued in his prophecy to reveal the final fall and destruction of Babylon in those days just preceding this time when the Lord in the day of His wrath would so shake the earth it would veer out of its established orbit: *"Behold, I will stir up the Medes against them, which shall not regard silver; and as for gold, they shall not delight in it. Their bows also shall dash the young men to pieces; and they shall have no pity on the fruit of the womb; their eye shall not spare children. And Babylon, the glory of kingdoms, the beauty of the Chaldees' excellency, shall be as when God overthrew Sodom and Gomorrah. It shall never be inhabited, neither shall it be dwelt in from generation to generation: neither shall the Arabian pitch tent there; neither shall the shepherds make their fold there."* (Isa. 13:17-20).

Again, remember that Isaiah saw the history of Babylon as one continuing scene without interruption, briefly seeing the Medes marching into the city, but proceeding right into the concluding scene when Babylon will be desolated in a massive holocaust very similar to the fiery judgment that consumed Sodom and Gomorrah. At the writing of this book, this judgment upon Babylon, or modern Iraq, is yet to come, though it may be very near.

The traditional Arabian was a nomad, moving from place to place to find pasture for his sheep and other livestock, because Arabia since the flood has been mostly a barren land. Thus, the Bedouins from Arabia have for thousands of years roamed the deserts from Libya to Iran. When we were in Babylon in 1978 a Bedouin tent was pitched on the outskirts of the city. So even when Babylon was covered with sand, Arabians continued to pitch their tents in the area. But Isaiah prophesied that after the final destruction, descriptive of a nuclear holocaust, no Bedouin would ever pitch tent there again.

Throughout the Book of Isaiah there are scattered references to the final fall and judgment upon Babylon, and we find this last warning in Isaiah 48:14, 20: "*. . . he will do his pleasure on Babylon, and his arm shall be on the Chaldeans . . . Go ye forth of Babylon, flee ye from the Chaldeans. . . .*"

Chapter Ten

Jeremiah Against Babylon

God revealed to Isaiah the rise and fall of Babylon one hundred years before Nebuchadnezzar destroyed Jerusalem and the Temple. However, the prophet Jeremiah lived in Judah during the time of the Babylonian invasion, and predicted by inspiration of the Holy Spirit the length of time that the Jews would be in captivity to Babylon: *"And this whole land shall be a desolation, and an astonishment; and these nations shall serve the king of Babylon seventy years. And it shall come to pass, when seventy years are accomplished, that I will punish the king of Babylon, and that nation, saith the Lord, for their iniquity, and the land of the Chaldeans, and will make it perpetual desolations"* (Jer. 25:11-12).

We know by history and Daniel 9:1-2 that the captivity of Judah by Babylon did last for seventy years, but the second part of the prophecy relating to the perpetual desolation of Babylon has not been fulfilled to this day. A more detailed and progressive, prophetic view of Babylonian history from the time of Nebuchadnezzar to the second coming of Jesus Christ was set forth by the prophet in Jeremiah 50 and 51. *"The word that the Lord spake against Babylon and against the land of the Chaldeans by Jeremiah the prophet. Declare ye among the nations, and publish, and set up a standard; publish, and conceal not: say, Babylon is taken, Bel is confounded, Merodach is broken in pieces; her idols are confounded, her images are broken in pieces. For out of the north there cometh up a nation against her, which shall make her land desolate, and none shall dwell therein: they shall remove, they shall depart, both men and beast. In those days, and in that time, saith the Lord, the children of Israel shall come, they and the children of Judah together, going and weeping: they shall go, and seek the Lord their God. They shall ask the way to Zion with their faces thitherward, saying, Come, and let us join ourselves to the Lord in a perpetual covenant that shall not be forgotten"* (Jer. 50:1-5).

It is evident from the beginning of Jeremiah's prophecy against Babylon that he was not speaking primarily about the Babylon of his day. The prophet understood that he was speaking of the distant future — "in those days, and in that time." Jeremiah understood that after seventy years a remnant would return from Babylon, but beyond that return, he must have understood about another return from all the world when the children of Israel and the children of Judah would both come weeping to the land seeking the Lord their God (Messiah) to make an everlasting covenant that would never be forgotten. This did not occur when the Jews came back from Babylon in the third and fourth centuries B.C. It will be in "those days" and in "that time," that the great desolation of Babylon, including the entire land of Chaldea, will take place. God has never forgiven the descendants of Esau for their crimes against Israel, and on a national basis, God has not forgiven Babylon.

"Remove out of the midst of Babylon, and go forth out of the land of the Chaldeans, and be as the he goats before the flocks. For, lo, I will raise and cause to come up against Babylon an assembly of great nations from the north country: and they shall set themselves in array against her; from thence she shall be taken: their arrows shall be as of a mighty expert man; none shall return in vain" (Jer. 50:8-9).

In these verses another warning is given to aliens in the land to get out before judgment falls. The signal for the eventual desolation of the entire land of Babylon is the assembling of the armies of great nations. The weaponry of these armies are arrows shot, or launched, by experts, indicating high technology. As a result of the arrows, it is not stretching the meaning of the scriptures to infer they will bring about the sudden desolation of Babylon as occurred at Sodom and Gomorrah. Have arrows shot from bows ever brought about the desolation of any nation? What kind of arrows must these be?

On page one of the August 18, 1990 *Jerusalem Post*, under the heading "Arrow Missile Tested," we read the following:

"At 3:35 p.m. the Arrow Missile [was] *shot into the sky at slightly under ten times the speed of sound. . . . The test proves the Arrow can be launched and can reach operational*

speed. . . . The U.S. Strategic Air Command is running the project on the American side, while Israel Aircraft Industries is building it here."

Israel has approximately one hundred atomic bombs and a dozen hydrogen bombs, according to common news media reports. It seems more than coincidental that Israel's latest missile program is called Arrow.

"Your mother shall be sore confounded; she that bare you shall be ashamed: behold, the hindermost of the nations shall be a wilderness, a dry land, and a desert. Because of the wrath of the Lord it shall not be inhabited, but it shall be wholly desolate: every one that goeth by Babylon shall be astonished, and hiss at all her plagues. Put yourselves in array against Babylon round about: all ye that bend the bow, shoot at her, spare no arrows: for she hath sinned against the Lord" (Jer. 50:12-14).

If Babylon is perhaps the United States, then the mother would be England. However, in light of the rise of Iraq and the rebuilding of the city of Babylon, the mother could refer to the Arab race and the Islamic religion. The Moslem leaders of Saudi Arabia, the homeland and foundation of Islam, have openly stated that they are ashamed of the Iraqis in that they have denied the faith and murdered their own brothers. As in other prophecies referring to the final destruction of Babylon, we see again in the preceding verses warnings about the coming desolation of that nation and the shooting of arrows by many nations to produce the extreme devastation. In verse twelve it should be noted that the prophet expresses surprise that the "hindermost" of nations would attract such opposition from the assembly of nations. According to *Webster's Dictionary*, hindermost means the lowest part, or the most posterior part, like the tail. Hindermost, if referring to the United States could mean the last of the great nations to rise, or if referring to Iraq, could mean a seemingly small and lowly nation.

And indeed, the world is amazed that a nation the size of California, with one-fifteenth the population of the United States, could suddenly endanger the major energy source of the world and command a worldwide mobilization. Jeremiah wonders that this lowest of nations would challenge an assembly of great nations, but this is exactly what occurred in the Middle East crisis of 1990. This little nation with only 17 million people challenged the will of the General Assembly of the United Nations.

"Cut off the sower from Babylon, and him that handleth the sickle in the time of harvest: for fear of the oppressing sword they shall turn every one to his people, and they shall flee every one to his own land" (Jer. 50:16).

At the time that Iraq invaded Kuwait, there were millions of workers, businessmen, and technicians from other nations in that little country. The oil-rich economy established a super-wealthy native and foreign elite who employed workers and household servants from the poor nations. In Iraq, millions from other countries had found work in the oil fields as well as the third largest military establishment in the world. While Iraq imports large quantities of certain types of food, the fertile land between the Tigris and Euphrates rivers produces most of the nation's vegetables. Because of the long war with Iran and the manpower shortage, farm workers came from Egypt, India, Pakistan, and other countries — 2 million from Egypt alone. With the invasion of Kuwait, these workers dropped their hammers, saws, brooms, plows, and hoes and fled westward to Jordan where they piled up on the desert border by the hundreds of thousands.

In the next few verses the prophetic scene merges the immediate future with the distant future, and then changes again to the very end of the age: *"And I will bring Israel again to his habitation, and he shall feed on Carmel and Bashan, and his soul shall be satisfied upon mount Ephraim and Gilead. In those days, and in that time, saith the Lord, the iniquity of Israel shall be sought for, and there shall be none; and the sins of Judah, and they shall not be found: for I will pardon them whom I reserve"* (Jer. 50:19-20).

Carmel, Bashan, and Mount Ephraim are a part of Israel today, as well as the northwest area of Gilead to the east of the lower part of Galilee. Bashan has not been occupied by Israel since the days of King Solomon, that is, until after the 1967 war. Bashan is today known as the Golan Heights. While these areas are occupied by Israelis today, the iniquity of Israel and the sins of Judah have not been pardoned, nor will they be until all Israel cries out to Jesus Christ, *". . . Blessed is he that cometh in the name of the Lord"*(Matt. 23:39). As mentioned by Jeremiah, it will be a part of Israel whom God will reserve to be pardoned from sin and enter into an everlasting covenant with God (Zech. 13:8-9).

"A sword is upon their horses, and upon their chariots, and upon all the mingled people that are in the midst of her; and they shall become as women: a sword is upon her treasures; and they shall be robbed . . . As God overthrew Sodom and Gomorrah and the neighbour cities thereof, saith the Lord; so shall no man abide there, neither shall any son of man dwell therein. Behold, a people shall come from the north, and a great nation, and many kings shall be raised up from the coasts of the earth. They shall hold the bow and the lance: they are cruel, and will not shew mercy: their voice shall roar like the sea, and they shall ride upon horses, every one put in array, like a man to the battle, against thee, O daughter of Babylon" (Jer. 50:37, 40-42).

The prophets often explained warfare in the last days in the common language and technology of their day. If they had named, or accurately described, tanks, airplanes, and other weapons of contemporary use, the Bible would have been discarded as the work of madmen. The prophet does say that the sounds of this great army would be like the roar of the sea — tanks driven by seven hundred horsepower and planes roaring through the sky. In these verses Jeremiah again refers to the mingled people who would be in Babylon at the time of judgment, and like Isaiah, Jeremiah compares the coming destruction of Babylon to that of Sodom and Gomorrah.

As to the alliance of nations that will come against Babylon, Jeremiah refers to a "people from the north." These people could be Turkey, NATO, or even Russia if it is to Russia's advantage to take part in the dividing of the spoils. Next, Jeremiah prophesies that "a great nation" will also come against Babylon, possibly a reference to the United States. Lastly, the prophet says that the armies of many other nations will join in when the time comes for Babylon's complete annihilation, and no mercy will be shown. Next, Jeremiah sees the king of Babylon as the armies of many nations gather against him: *"The king of Babylon hath heard the report of them, and his hands waxed feeble: anguish took hold of him, and pangs as of a woman in travail. Behold, he shall come up like a lion from the swelling of Jordan unto the habitation of the strong . . . At the noise of the taking of Babylon the earth is moved, and the cry is heard among the nations"* (Jer. 50:43-44, 46).

Nebuchadnezzar built up the city-state of Babylon into a world empire. He emerged from an obscure beginning to become the most powerful man in the world. He was a cruel, proud, and egotistical man. He burned victims who refused to worship him as a god. Saddam Hussein also rose from an obscure background. He got his start in politics as a revolutionary against the government of Iraq. He escaped execution by fleeing to Egypt where he continued his education. After his political friends gained power in Iraq, Saddam returned and quickly rose in political stature. As Iraq's chief security officer, he hanged nine Jews on the streets of Baghdad in 1969. Although he wielded much power in the socialist government of Iraq, and was instrumental in promoting the rebuilding of Babylon, he was not made the absolute dictator. He quickly identified those he could not trust in his own party, and it is reported that he personally shot everyone that was singled out. Saddam, on one occasion, shot a top general for daring to suggest an alternative military action. There is little doubt, according to CIA intelligence reports, that if President Bush would not have taken immediate action, the Iraqi dictator would have invaded Saudi Arabia and possibly become even greater than Nebuchadnezzar.

But in prophesying about the king of Babylon that would be destroyed like Sodom and Gomorrah, Jeremiah did not say Nebuchadnezzar, but rather "the king of Babylon." Saddam Hussein has indeed come up like a lion, like the swelling of the Jordan at flood stage. He has gained the attention and fear of the world, but Jeremiah prophesied that when the chips were down, the king of Babylon would become as weak and helpless as a woman in childbirth. While Jeremiah's prophecy about the king of Babylon could refer to Belshazzar at the taking of old Babylon by the Medes and the Persians, the prophecy more aptly applies to the present dictator.

The concluding prophecy against Babylon in Jeremiah 50 foretells that when the assembly of nations finally attack and destroy it, even the earth will shake and the cry of the people will be heard within the nations. The earth moving seems to indicate tremendous atomic explosions, and with modern television, the cry of the people could be heard in the nations of the world.

"Thus saith the Lord; Behold, I will raise up against Babylon, and against them that dwell in the midst of them that rise up against me, a destroying wind; And will send unto Babylon fanners, that shall fan her, and shall empty her land: for in the day of trouble they shall be against her round about . . . Flee out of the midst of Babylon, and deliver every man his soul: be not cut off in her iniquity; for this is the time of the Lord's vengeance; he will render unto her a recompence" (Jer. 51:1-2, 6).

The most feared weapon Saddam Hussein has is poison gas, mainly mustard gas and nerve gas, and he has shown his willingness to use it against even his own people. Poison gas has not been used since World War I, and there were stories reported about how the Germans would unleash poison gas, but then the wind would change and their own soldiers would be killed. The destroying wind prophesied against Babylon by Jeremiah could be poison gas sweeping across the nation. If air attacks were to destroy the poison gas factories and weapons before being launched or used, such a thing could easily happen. This is the reason the prophet again warns foreigners in Babylon to flee before this destroying wind comes.

"Nebuchadnezzar the king of Babylon hath devoured me, he hath crushed me, he hath made me an empty vessel, he hath swallowed me up like a dragon . . . The

violence done to me and to my flesh be upon Babylon . . . and my blood upon the inhabitants of Chaldea, shall Jerusalem say. Therefore thus saith the Lord; Behold, I will plead thy cause, and take vengeance for thee . . ." (Jer. 51:34-36).

It may appear cruel and unjust for such a terrible judgment to be pronounced upon any nation, especially by a loving and merciful God. But God is not only merciful, not willing that any should perish, He is also a just God. Babylon has never as yet paid for the rape, plunder, and destruction of Jerusalem and the Temple some twenty-five hundred years ago. We know the Word of God declares that whosoever defiles the Temple, him will God destroy. And so God has said to Israel through Jeremiah the prophet, do not concern yourself about vengeance upon Babylon, I will take care of it in my own way and time.

"And thou shalt say, Thus shall Babylon sink, and shall not rise from the evil that I will bring upon her: and they shall be weary. Thus far are the words of Jeremiah" (Jer. 51:64).

Chapter Eleven

John Against Babylon

Besides end-time judgments pronounced against Babylon in Isaiah, Jeremiah, and the Book of Revelation, others are scattered throughout the Bible. For example, we read in Ezekiel 32:11-15, *"For thus saith the Lord God; The sword of the king of Babylon shall come upon thee. By the swords of the mighty will I cause thy multitude to fall, the terrible of the nations, all of them: and they shall spoil the pomp of Egypt, and all the multitude thereof shall be destroyed. I will destroy also all the beasts thereof from beside the great waters; neither shall the foot of man trouble them any more, nor the hoofs of beasts trouble them. Then will I make their waters deep, and cause their rivers to run like oil, saith the Lord God."*

Here in the extremity of the age, two old enemies, Egypt and Babylon, face each other across the border between Arabia and Iraq. It seems apparent from the prophecy of Ezekiel that even though Babylon will be desolated like Sodom and Gomorrah, the king of Babylon will be involved in the desolation of Egypt. As a result of this judgment that will come upon both nations, their rivers will run like oil. Remarkable! In the event of war, millions of barrels of oil could run into the Tigris and Euphrates rivers, fulfilling this prophecy. An expressed concern of many nations who depend upon Middle East oil is the purposed or accidental rupture of the oil fields in Iraq, Kuwait, Iran, and Saudi Arabia.

More details about the coming desolation of Egypt are given in Ezekiel 29:8-12, *"Therefore thus saith the Lord God; Behold, I will bring a sword upon thee, and cut off man and beast out of thee. And the land of Egypt shall be desolate and waste; and they shall know that I am the Lord: because he hath said, The river is mine, and I have made it. Behold, therefore I am against thee, and against thy rivers, and I will make the land of Egypt utterly waste and desolate, from the tower of Syene even unto the border of Ethiopia. No foot of man shall pass through it, nor foot of beast shall pass through it, neither shall it be inhabited forty years. And I will make the land of Egypt desolate in the midst of the countries that are desolate, and her cities among the cities that are laid waste shall be desolate forty years. . . ."*

Not only will Babylon be desolated like Sodom and Gomorrah, but many of the cities of Egypt will be made desolate in the same manner. Also, Egypt will be in the middle of many other cities and nations in the Middle East that will be made desolate so that for forty years even a dog will not be able to pass through and live. This prophecy was given to Ezekiel over twenty-five hundred years ago, yet there is no more accurate description of what will happen if an atomic war occurs in that part of the world. In other prophecies relating to the judgment of nations in the Day of the Lord we are informed that Damascus (Syria) will be a ruinous heap; the mountains of Lebanon will be on fire; Arabia will be scorched with terrible heat; etc. According to Daniel and Jesus Christ, the time of great desolation will occur when the Antichrist breaks his treaty with Israel and commits the "Abomination of Desolation."

The fiery destruction of Babylon is the apex of Great Tribulation judgments, because it is the religion of Babylon that has deceived the world through a multitude of deceptions. Even while the ancient city of Babylon lay underneath the sands of the Euphrates, religious Babylon, also called Mystery Babylon, permeated the world under a multitude of occultic worships. In these last days, the New Age movement with its many-faceted forms of mysterious worships in crystals, astrology, incantations, meditations, gods of illuminations and ascended masters, is an assortment of Babylonian mysteries.

Martin Luther, after going to Rome and witnessing the corruption, opulence, and blasphemy of the Vatican proclaimed that the Catholic Church was Mystery Babylon and Pope Leo was the Antichrist. Many Protestant theologians and ministers have agreed with Luther, and today when traveling in predominantly Roman Catholic countries and visiting cathedrals like Notre Dame in Paris, St. Peter's of Rome, and the Cathedral of Toledo near Madrid, we are tempted to join with others in making a similar comparison between the Vatican and the great whore of Revelation 17. The wealth on display in these cathedrals and monasteries (jewels, silver, robes, and idols of solid gold statues weighing up to a thousand pounds) in the midst of extreme poverty sickens our very soul. Hislop, in *The Two Babylons*, makes a good case for the Catholic Church carrying on the Babylonian priesthood, and as previously noted, the symbol of Nimrod, the obelisk, stands in front of St. Peter's in Rome and in front of Sophia Hagia in Istanbul (Constantinople).

Let us assume that Roman Catholicism is the Mystery Babylon of Revelation and the pope is the false prophet. How would this theoretic possibility fit into the religious scenario of the tribulation? In light of what we know today, with the United Nations finally reaching its envisioned potential during the 1990 Middle East crisis, what if the U.N. were to appoint a central religious agency to coincide with the international political authority? This, as viewed from a one-world perspective, would certainly be desirable. Religious fanaticism in the Moslem world, Orthodox Judaism, Hinduism, Buddhism, and apostate Christendom would need to be polarized and directed toward a single humanistic goal — peace on earth!

Would all the different religions, sects, and cults have to concede, adhere to, or profess a unity of doctrine or liturgy? Not at all. The only common expectation would be to agree to pursue a goal of world peace under the leadership of a single authority. The most recognized single religious personality in the world who would project the image of world peace for the good of all mankind, would without controversy be the pope. Mystery Babylon, the culmination of the religion of Nimrod, is not envisioned by John to be a single entity, but the "mother of harlots," the incorporation of many harlots into one family. While we do not profess to know every turn in the course of coming events, and neither do we say without qualification that the Roman Catholic Church will be the shelter for the church of the false prophet, in light of current world developments we are beginning to understand how it could happen. All major world religions, including the New Age movement, are waiting for their own particular messiah. It would be a readily acceptable announcement to declare one personality as a god of all who will take his mark and follow him to a world order of peace and prosperity. Mystery Babylon fulfills the plan of Nimrod to bring all races, languages, and nations back into a common world where all divisions of mankind are unified into the worship of one political head (Rev. 13).

The enforcement of the mark of the beast upon humanity and the worship of the Antichrist as god concludes the need for a religious order. God puts into the mind of the beast a plan to destroy Mystery Babylon (Rev. 17:17). The annihilation of the world congress of religions, with all offices, priests, monks, ministers, etc., must take place soon after the Antichrist sits in the Temple of God showing himself to all the world as God.

National Babylon is not to be confused with Mystery Babylon, even though there may be a religious identification common to both. While the judgment of the great whore seems to be foretold to occur at the beginning of the second half of the Great Tribulation, the destruction of national Babylon is somewhat more difficult to place. From the Old Testament it appears certain that Babylon is to be destroyed and made desolate in the great and terrible day of the Lord — the tribulation period — within seven years of the second coming of Jesus Christ. That the destruction and judgment of Babylon is to occur before the battle of Armageddon appears obvious because Babylon is not listed among those nations whose armies will be decimated with the brightness of His coming. And while John seems to indicate the destruction of national Babylon near the end of the Great Tribulation, in Revelation 14:8, he indicates the same judgment to occur in the first half.

Many have erred in basing prophetic chronology on current events that appear to have pregnant eschatological promises. But from what we overtly see taking place in the Middle East and the respective role of the super powers in that developing conflict, we can understand how a sudden and massive desolation of Iraq could trigger an invasion by Russia down through Turkey and over the Golan Heights into Israel.

An increasing percentage of the world's wealth goes to the nations of the Persian Gulf for oil. How long it will take, or exactly what events must transpire, to fulfill the conditions and situations set forth in describing the judgment of Babylon like Sodom and Gomorrah cannot be fully determined at this time. But for the first time, we who are comparing the signs of the times with the prophetic Word may be reasonably assured that the long shadows of the coming great and terrible day of the Lord are being cast upon the desert sands of Saudi Arabia, Iraq, Iran, Syria, Jordan, and Egypt. This we know for certain, the Apostle John saw the coming destruction of Babylon as taking place in one hour on a particular day. God knows the day the destruction of Babylon is to take place, and in 1 Thessalonians 5:1-5, Paul admonished that Christians should not let the day of the Lord come as a thief in the night.

Christians today have many reasons to expect the coming of the Lord at any time. Therefore, *". . . let us, who are of the day, be sober, putting on the breastplate of faith and love; and for an helmet, the hope of salvation"* (1 Thess. 5:8).

Chapter Twelve

The World Beyond Babylon

On a cold March morning, sixty-two-year-old Gerald Vincent Bull was shot to death by assassins as he left his apartment building in Brussels. Such assassinations are common to the world of the 1990s, but there was something very unusual about this one. Bull had the proven record of being a ballistic and ordinance genius who had performed valuable service to the United States, Canada, and Israel. But at the time of his death in Brussels, the artillery genius was working for Saddam Hussein to develop a supergun called "Project Babylon."

In World War I the Germans developed three enormous howitzers with a range of seventy-four miles. These guns were used to lob shells into Paris, but they disappeared after the war. Even in World War II the largest artillery guns had a range of only twenty-five miles. However, in 1973 Gerald Vincent Bull sold Israel fifty thousand shells that would bombard Damascus from the Golan Heights, but these were never used. Evidently, Israel still has them in storage. Bull was also reported in *Fame* magazine to have helped Israel neutralize electronic equipment at the raid on Entebbe.

In 1965 the daughter of the German who designed

the Paris Gun (also called Big Bertha) provided Bull with the blueprints of the World War I artillery monster. Subsequently, Bull went to Barbados, where he could operate in relative secrecy, and came up with a one hundred ten foot gun that would propel a two hundred pound shell a distance of twenty-five hundred miles. Another model was developed that would propel a twelve hundred pound projectile a distance of six hundred miles. The United States and Canada turned down Bull's offer to incorporate such weapons into their armed forces, favoring instead already developed rockets.

Bitterly disappointed, Bull found a ready customer in Saddam Hussein. According to the *Jerusalem Post* of September 15, 1990, Bull designed a 155-howitzer that was made in Austria, far superior to anything the United States has. Three hundred of these artillery weapons are now in Iraq and will be used against Americans in the event of war. Bull was also financed by Saddam Hussein to develop three long-range multi-purpose guns that would hit targets anywhere in the Middle East, including Jerusalem. These guns would fire conventional explosives, poison gas, or nuclear warheads. Contracts were let in seven European nations and the parts were then sent to Iraq to be assembled. But the clandestine plot began to break down simply because it was too diversified. While forty-four parts of the first long-range howitzer did reach Baghdad, the remaining eight essential parts were intercepted. Bull was assassinated by either CIA, Mossad, or Iraqi agents.

Only our imagination can contemplate what horror

Saddam Hussein could have created had he been able to complete the assembling of these huge, long-range guns. It seems likely, from the interception of nuclear bomb pieces in London bound for Iraq, that atomic shells were contemplated. A prototype of one of the guns, called "Baby Babylon," was test-fired at Mosul, just across the Tigris River at the site of the old city of Nineveh. Of what use this artillery weapon will be to Iraq in the future is unknown.

Besides the NATO nations of Europe, the United States, Russia, China, and Israel, at least a dozen Third World nations have the ability to develop and deliver mass destructive weapons. Saddam Hussein is just an example of what could happen in almost any nation where a strong man takes control of the government with ambitions to become a world dictator.

The United Nations was established as a viable international organization in June 1945 in San Francisco. The U.N. was actually a rebirth of the old League of Nations, and for all intents and purposes, other than being a forum for international griping and complaints, the organization has been no more effective than its former model. It has, however, provided large salaries and plush homes for international loafers, mostly at the expense of American taxpayers.

The United Nations was founded as "an international organization dedicated to the maintenance of international peace and security, and composed of nations subscribing to the principles and obligations enumerated in the Charter of the United Nations" (Funk and Wagnall Encyclopedia). As stated in the charter, member nations were to settle their differences through peaceful negotiations within the office of the U.N. rather than resorting to war or force of arms. During the time the U.N. has been in existence, there have been no world wars of the scope of World War I and World War II. However, there have been a multitude of lesser wars and revolutions: Korean War, Vietnam War, Afghanistan War, Cuba, Angola, Nicaragua, Lebanon, three wars between Israel and the Arab Alliance, China, Cambodia, etc. Perhaps the main reason for no extensive international war has been the fear of nuclear annihilation.

However, when Saddam Hussein threatened the world's major oil supply, with a resulting threat of financial shockwaves that could have overturned the international banking system, the United Nations finally acted in unison to condemn the aggression and endorsed United States' plans to stand up against the bully of Baghdad. Some of the nations like Egypt and Syria are supporting the U.S. position, along with some military units, simply because they hate anyone in the Arab world standing taller than they stand. Russia has given lip service to the U.N. effort, but at the same time opposes military action and keeps several thousand technicians and military advisors in Iraq to insure that the United States does not use military action. What will happen relative to this thorny issue may only be revealed by time. But the one issue that finally brought the U.N. to a unified position was not to save the peace, but rather, to save the oil.

On September 11, 1990, the President of the United States, George Bush, appeared on television before the entire world and made the following announcement:

> " *A new partnership of nations has emerged. . . . Out of these troubled times, a New World Order can emerge. . . . A hundred generations have searched for this elusive path to peace, while a thousand wars raged across the span of human endeavor. Today that new world is struggling to be born . . . a world where the rule of law supplants the rule of the jungle; a world in which nations recognize the shared responsibility for freedom and justice; a world where the strong respect the rights of the weak. . . . This is the vision I shared with President Gorbachev in Helsinki.*

Almost two thousand years ago another man stood on Mount Olivet in Jerusalem, and looking forward in time to the very end of the age, He said: *". . . Take heed that no man deceive you . . . ye shall hear of wars and rumours of wars: see that ye be not troubled: for all these things must come to pass, but the end is not yet. For nation shall rise against nation, and kingdom against kingdom: and there shall be famines, and pestilences, and earthquakes, in divers places. All these are the beginning of sorrows"* (Matt. 24:4-8).

Even so-called conservative voices like the *National Review* have been caught up in the fantasy of the New

World Order:

> *"New international order . . . that the post-Cold War should, as far as possible, be one of peace and stability. This is not global altruism. As a world power with economic presence in all continents, the U.S. has strong interests in the international order that trade and overseas investment require."*

Patrick Buchanan in an editorial that appeared in the *Daily Oklahoman* of September 15, 1990, said of the above statement that appeared in *National Review*:

> *"Excuse me, this is not conservatism; it is Trilateralism, the foreign policy of David Rockefeller. . . ."*

The Council on Foreign Relations, the Trilateral Commission, Club of Rome, Common Market, international communism, United Nations, international bankers, World Council of Churches, Roman Catholic Church, New Age movement, and dozens of other pseudo-political and religious organizations and groups we could name, are all hailing the facade of world peace through world government in the wake of the U.N. embargo against Iraq. But each group or organization sees in a New World Order an opportunity to attain to its own economic, political, or religious goal.

In reference to the illusionary alliance between the

United States and Russia within the framework of a New World Order, an editorial on page 27 of the September 17, 1990 edition of *Newsweek* observed:

> *"Washington's real ally is not the Soviet Union, but Gorbachev himself. In a few years — or even a few weeks — he could fall from power. . . . In the end, the new reapportionment between old rivals relies on personal diplomacy — and that makes it inherently fragile."*

From the prophetic Word of God we can know:

- National Babylon will be destroyed in a fiery judgment
- Israel will be forced to sign a peace treaty that will concern the land
- Russia will invade Israel over the Golan Heights
- There will be a world political order
- There will be a world religious order
- The world religious order will be destroyed by the world political order
- The leader of the world political order will break the treaty with Israel
- The armies from out of all nations will move against Israel
- The international army will be destroyed by Jesus Christ at His coming
- Jesus Christ will then take the government of all the world upon Himself

- There will be peace and prosperity in all the world for one thousand years

There are many other events foretold in the Bible that will occur within the seven-year period preceding the return of Jesus Christ, and except for the last three items listed, we cannot say for sure in which order the others will occur.

We are in no way predicting the rapture of the church and the beginning of the tribulation in the immediate future. There has been far too much date-setting for the Lord's return in recent years. However, there are strong and striking parallels in the developing situation in the Middle East today with events God declares must come to pass before Jesus Christ returns. *If*, and again we say *if*, the gathering of the armies of many nations from the coasts of the world against Iraq is that which is described by Isaiah, Jeremiah, and other prophets, then the following suggested scenario would seem reasonable:

The Arab nations, as well as Russia, will demand that the Palestine issue and the West Bank be a part of the overall Middle East settlement before military action is considered against Iraq. Saudi Arabia has claimed the right to delay military action by all foreign armies in the country until the government of Saudi Arabia gives permission. Israel will be forced to sign a general agreement or covenant to satisfy other nations within the United Nations. In return, Israel will be given certain concessions also, including the right to build a tabernacle or a Temple on, or near, the Temple Mount.

Iraq still refuses to withdraw from Kuwait and is destroyed in one day.

Russia seizes the opportunity to gain the support of all Arab nations and claim the Middle East oil fields by moving a huge army down through Syria, over the Golans, toward Israel. That army is destroyed as described in Ezekiel 38 and 39.

World government is established, supported in union by all religions and headed by a spiritual leader.

The man elected by the United Nations to be the world president moves against Israel for not becoming a part of the world religious system. Then the world president sits in the Temple and declares himself to be god.

The remnant of Israel who have refused to worship the world president as god, and those who are not killed, escape southward through the mountains to Petra.

While the multitude of world religious leaders within the unified religious system are willing to accept the world president and have helped bring him to power, when he forces everyone in the world to worship him as god and receive a mark in their forehead or their hand, they rebel and the entire Babylonish religious system of the world is destroyed.

The world president reigns as Antichrist for the last half of the tribulation period and marshalls all the armies of the world in Israel to keep him in power. Jesus Christ returns as King of kings and Lord of lords with the armies of Heaven, and all the forces of Antichrist are destroyed at Armageddon.

Jesus Christ establishes His own government, appoints His own judges and governors over the nations, and reigns from David's throne in Jerusalem. Mankind will at last have peace on earth, the law will be enforced from Jerusalem, crime will be at a minimum, and the ecology will return to its pristine state.

President George Bush said at his meeting with Mikhail Gorbachev in Finland:

"If the nations of the world, acting together, continue as they have been, we will set in place the cornerstone of an international order more peaceful than any that we have known."

In the events taking shape in the Persian Gulf Crisis, we agree with President Bush that it is time to lay the cornerstone of a new international order. But the cornerstone that will be laid is not the United Nations cornerstone, but Jesus Christ Himself, the Stone that will strike the image of all Gentile power and authority at the Battle of Armageddon (Dan. 2).

"*. . . Behold, I lay in Sion a chief corner stone, elect, precious: and he that believeth on him shall not be confounded . . . the stone which the builders disallowed, the same is made the head of the corner, And a stone of stumbling, and a rock of offence . . .*" (1 Pet. 2:6-8).